# New American STREAMLINE

### BERNARD HARTLEY & PETER VINEY

## DESTINATIONS

**An intensive American English series for advanced students**
Workbook B
Units 41–80
REVISED BY IRENE FRANKEL

## Oxford University Press

Oxford University Press

198 Madison Avenue
New York, NY 10016 USA

Walton Street
Oxford OX2 6DP  England

OXFORD is a trademark of Oxford University Press.

ISBN 0-19-434839-3

Based on the American adaptation by Flamm/Northam
Authors and Publishers Services, Inc.

Project Editor: Ken Mencz
Editor: Shirley Brod
Associate Production Editor: Annmarie Lockhart
Picture Researcher: Paul Hahn
Production Manager: Abram Hall
Design by: Design Five

Cover illustration by: Pete Kelly

*Illustrations and realia by:* Carlos Castellanos,
Gary Hallgren, Veronica Jones, Gerard Cortinez,
Tom Powers, Terry Wight

The publishers would like to thank the following for
their permission to reproduce photographs:
Simon Baigelman
*Liaison International:* Tony Cordoza, Arvind Garg,
Roy Gumpel, Mark Lewis, Charles Nes, Joe Polillio,
Sotographs, Aaron Strong
*H. Armstrong Roberts:* C. Bayer/Mauritius,
Frauke/Mauritius
*International Stock:* Peter Russell Clemens
*The Stock Market:* John Feingersh, Mugshots

For permission to reprint copyright material,
the publisher wishes to make the following
acknowledgment:
Truman Capote, excerpt from
*Music for Chameleons.* Copyright © 1980 Truman Capote.
Reprinted by permission of Random House, Inc.

Printing (last digit) 10 9 8 7 6 5 4 3 2 1

Printed in Canada

# TO THE TEACHER

*Workbook B* of *New American Streamline: Destinations* consists of forty units. Each unit relates directly to the corresponding unit in *New American Streamline: Destinations,* Units 41–80.

The Workbook is an optional component of the series, designed to provide language summaries and additional written exercises. It may be used in the following ways:

1. In more extensive courses as additional classroom material, providing extra oral practice and written reinforcement and consolidation of the basic core material in the Student Book.
2. As homework material in more intensive situations.

The Workbook should only be used after full oral practice of the corresponding unit in the Student Book. The language summaries provide material for review.

Another workbook is available for Units 1–40 of the Student Book, under the title *Workbook A.*

*Bernard Hartley*
*Peter Viney*
*Irene Frankel*

# Unit 41

## Exercise 1

Read these instructions for brewing a pot of rich drip coffee and number them 1–6 in the correct order.

Grind fresh coffee beans very finely.

When the water boils, remove it from the heat and wait two minutes.

Serve with sugar and milk or cream, only if desired.

Begin by filling a kettle with fresh cold water, and put it on the stove to boil.

Measure coffee into paper or metal filter—two tablespoons per six-ounce cup.

Slowly pour the hot water over the coffee.

## Exercise 2

Read this recipe for Southern fried chicken. Write out a recipe from your country or region in the same way.

### SOUTHERN FRIED CHICKEN
*(Serves 4)*

| | |
|---|---|
| 1 four-pound chicken or | 1 tablespoon salt |
| 2 two-pound chickens | Black pepper |
| 1/2 quart buttermilk | Vegetable oil for frying |
| 1 tablespoon poultry seasoning | 3 cups flour |
| (mixture of thyme, sage) | |

In a large bowl, combine the buttermilk and poultry seasoning, 1/2 tablespoon of salt and 1/2 cup of flour. Mix well. Place remaining 2 1/2 cups of flour and 1/2 tablespoon of salt with pepper to taste in another large bowl or baking pan. Have the chicken cut in frying pieces. Dip the pieces in the buttermilk batter, then roll them in the flour. Heat oil in a large heavy skillet. You will need plenty of oil; it should be about 1 1/2 inches deep in the pan. When it is bubbly hot but not burning, add the chicken pieces and cook them on all sides until they are dark golden brown, about 20 to 25 minutes. Do not allow the oil to burn; adjust heat as you go along. Turn the chicken pieces several times, raising the heat a little before each turn (to seal the batter), then lowering it. When the chicken is tender and done through, remove and drain on paper towels. Serve while still hot with mashed potatoes and a green vegetable, such as spinach or green beans.

## Exercise 3

Make a list of 20 items (not food or drink) that you might find in a kitchen.

1. ...................................
2. ...................................
3. ...................................
4. ...................................
5. ...................................
6. ...................................
7. ...................................
8. ...................................
9. ...................................
10. ...................................
11. ...................................
12. ...................................
13. ...................................
14. ...................................
15. ...................................
16. ...................................
17. ...................................
18. ...................................
19. ...................................
20. ...................................

## Exercise 4

You have been offered a four-course meal. You can have anything you want. Write out the menu you would choose.

1st course ..........................................................................

..............................................................................................

2nd course .........................................................................

..............................................................................................

3rd course ..........................................................................

..............................................................................................

4th course ..........................................................................

..............................................................................................

## Exercise 5

Ask a friend these questions, and write down his/her answers.

1. What time do you usually have

   A. breakfast? ................................................................

   B. lunch? .......................................................................

   C. dinner? ......................................................................

2. Which is your biggest meal of the day?

   ..........................................................................................

3. Do you ever snack between meals?

   ..........................................................................................

4. Is there anything that you really cannot eat or drink?

   ..........................................................................................

5. What's your favorite food?

   ..........................................................................................

## Exercise 6

Make a list of *everything* that you ate and drank yesterday. Compare your list with a friend's list.

# Unit 42

## Language Summary

| I wish I | was there. |
|----------|------------|
|          | wasn't here. |
|          | was working there. |
|          | wasn't working here. |
|          | had / a car. |
|          | didn't have |
|          | didn't have (to do this). |

| I wish I | could (do that). |
|----------|------------------|
|          | 'd (done that). |
|          | had |
|          | hadn't |
|          | worked there. |
|          | didn't work here. |

## Exercise 1

Gary is 19. He's just read about Mike Ross in the newspaper. This is Mike Ross. *I wish I was Mike Ross.*

Write more sentences.

1. He's a millionaire.
2. He's been to 80 countries.
3. He lives in Samoa.
4. He has houses in Los Angeles and New York.
5. He can run five miles.
6. He's getting married to Pamela Moss.

## Exercise 2

Read the article about Mike Ross again. Write five sentences for Gary, beginning with *I wish…*

1. rock star
2. 19 gold albums
3. sing and dance for three hours
4. six cars
5. a Ferrari

## Exercise 3

Gary asked three people this question:
*"Do you wish you were a millionaire?"*
One said, *"Yes, I do."* Another said, *"No, I don't."* The third said, *"I am a millionaire!"*

Look at Exercises 1 and 2. Write six questions, and give *true* answers.

---

*Daily Post*

### People in the News
**A birthday present for the man who has everything!**

What do you give to a man who has everything? Millionaire rock star **Mike Ross** celebrated his 38th birthday last week. Mike, who sings with **The Tumbling Dice,** has been one of the world's most popular rock artists for nearly 20 years. During that time, he's been to more than 80 different countries and has made 19 gold albums—records that sold more than a million copies each.

Mike lives in Samoa, but also maintains houses in Los Angeles and New York. He can still sing and dance throughout the group's three-hour stage show, and stays in shape by jogging. He runs five miles before breakfast every day. Next month he's getting married to supermodel **Pamela Moss**. She must have thought for a long time about his birthday present. After all, he owns six cars, and usually drives a Ferrari. Her present was certainly different. She gave him a pair of pet leopards!

## Exercise 4

Mike Ross was interviewed recently by Music TV, a cable television channel. Here are some of the things he said:

1. "I'd like to be 19 again!"
2. "I have to travel all the time. I don't like it."
3. "I get bored singing the same songs all the time."
4. "I'm getting married to Pamela. She's very beautiful, but she's very young."
5. "I'm fed up with living in the tropics."
6. "I'm tired of being a rock star."
7. "I'm sick of having lots of money."
8. "I hate running—but I have to stay in shape for the stage shows."

9. "I don't like having six cars. I'd like to travel on an ordinary city bus, but I'm too famous."
10. "When I was 19, I could have had a job in a bank, married the girl next door, and bought a nice little house. I'm sorry I didn't. I think I would have been happier."

Look at the things Mike said.

*He wishes he was 19 again.*
*He wishes he didn't have to travel.*

Now write eight more sentences with *wish* like the examples.

## Exercise 5

Look at the Language Summary. Write down eight things that *you* wish.

# Unit 43

## Language Summary

| I wish they | had<br>hadn't | gone there. | | If I'd done this, | that would have happened.<br>I would be … now. |

| I regret<br>I'm sorry | doing that.<br>it happened. |

---

## Exercise 1

Look at the list of high school subjects. Think about the previous school year or when you were in school. Check the boxes next to the subjects you took.

## Exercise 2

Look at these examples.

*I wish I hadn't taken Latin.* or *I'm glad I took Latin.* or *I wish I'd taken Latin.* or *I'm glad I didn't take Latin.*

Write true sentences about the subjects in the list.

## Exercise 3

Look at these sentences.

**A.** *I wish I hadn't taken Latin because it was boring, and I'll never have to use it.*

**B.** *I'm glad I took Latin because it has helped me to study other languages.*

**C.** *I wish I'd taken Latin. It would have been useful in college.*

**D.** *I'm glad I didn't take Latin. I think it would have been a waste of time.*

Look at the sentences you wrote in Exercise 2. Choose six, and write them out again, adding reasons.

## Exercise 4

I bought a calculator. It didn't work.
*I wish I hadn't bought it.*

Continue.

**1.** My friends went to New York. I didn't go.

......................................................................

**2.** I failed the test.

......................................................................

**3.** I was very rude to her yesterday.

......................................................................

**4.** I never played sports at school.

......................................................................

**5.** I had to take two history courses in school.

......................................................................

**6.** I chose the wrong job.

......................................................................

| School Subjects | | | |
|---|---|---|---|
| Algebra | | Latin | |
| Art | | Modern foreign language | |
| Biology | | Music | |
| Calculus | | Physical education | |
| Chemistry | | Physics | |
| Computer studies | | Plane geometry | |
| Drama | | Solid geometry | |
| Earth science | | Speech | |
| English | | Trigonometry | |
| Health education | | Typing | |
| Home economics (cooking or sewing) | | World history | |
| Industrial arts (woodworking or metal shop) | | Your language | |

## Exercise 5

I bought a calculator. It didn't work. *I regret buying it.*

Look at Exercise 4. Write six sentences, with "*I regret (doing) …*" or "*I regret not (doing)…*"

## Exercise 6

Think about the last year. Write three sentences with "*I regret (doing) …*" three with "*I don't regret doing…*"  and three with "*I'm sorry I didn't…*"

## Exercise 7

I'm very tired today. *I wish I wasn't.*
I went to bed late last night. *I wish I hadn't.*

Respond to the following sentences in the same way.

**1.** I didn't set the alarm.

......................................................................

**2.** It didn't go off.

......................................................................

**3.** I arrived late.

......................................................................

**4.** Now I can't concentrate on my work.

......................................................................

**5.** I feel terrible!

......................................................................

**6.** I don't understand anything.

......................................................................

**7.** I'm bored.

......................................................................

# LETTERS FROM OUR READERS

*Last month we asked our readers to tell us about their ambitions and dreams.*
*Lots of you wrote in! Here are three of your letters.*

**They say that every small child** wants to be a train engineer. I suppose that might have been true in the days of steam trains, but it's pretty hard to get excited about an electric train. Personally, I always wanted to be a pilot. I used to spend hours at the local airport with my brother, writing down the plane registrations. I knew everything there was to know about planes! When I was twelve I began to realize that the thick glasses I had to wear would make that ambition impossible. It's always a shock when you first realize that wishes don't always come true! It's funny. I really can't stand flying now. I often have to travel in my job ... I'm a marketing consultant ... and I suppose I'm sick of flying. I'm still a collector, but now it's china ornaments, not plane registrations. I think I've become something of an expert on 19th-century English china. I'd really like to write a book about it. I think that would be my biggest ambition!

*Anna Pollack*

**When I was a kid** I had just one dream. I used to imagine myself running out onto the field at the Super Bowl, a football under my arm ... the quarterback of the team! I'd spend hours practicing. I used to collect autographs too. I'd hang around before a game and try to get the players to sign a souvenir program when they got out of their cars. Programs! That's another thing. My bedroom was full of dusty sports programs. I used to swap them with other kids at school. I work in a shoe store now. All the little kids come in with their moms and dads, trying on football shoes. They get so excited. I can remember doing the same thing. I've lost interest in football nowadays. I prefer fooling around in my workshop in the garage. I make children's toys. You know, wooden ones. I really wish I could do it for a living ... full-time. Maybe one day I'll be able to.

*Howard Skinner*

**When I was about seven,** the circus came to our town and I still remember what a strong impression it made on me. I loved all the characters I saw and I had dreamed of running away to join them. I seriously considered all the possibilities: lion tamer, juggler, acrobat, trapeze artist; but in the end I decided to be a clown. I can remember spending long hours at my mother's dressing-table, putting on make-up to create a clown's face and then making faces in front of the mirror. Unfortunately I never ran away to join the circus. I dropped out of school when I was 16 and started working. I'm working now as a mechanic in a large garage—I suppose that's a bit of a circus sometimes! I'd like my own place one day, nothing big, just to be my own boss. On weekends I like to get away from everything. I spend hours and hours fishing by a river or a lake, just watching my float. I don't really mind if I don't catch anything, though I get a big thrill if I do! As soon as I could walk, my father used to take me with him, made me a rod, and I suppose that's how I've spent my spare time ever since.

*Tim Genovese*

## Exercise 1

Read the three letters, and complete the chart.

| Name | Childhood ambition | Childhood hobbies | Present occupation | Present hobbies | Ambition now |
|------|--------------------|--------------------|--------------------|-----------------|--------------|
| Anna Pollack | | | | | |
| Howard Skinner | | | | | |
| Tim Genovese | | | | | |

## Exercise 2

Write a paragraph about your childhood hobbies and ambitions, and your hobbies and ambitions now.

# Unit 45

## Language Summary

| He | is the one | who | does | that. |
|------|------------|-------|------|-------|
| She | | that | did | |
| It | | which | | |
| That | | that | | |
| Those | are the ones | who | do | it. |
| They | | which | did | |
| | | that | | |

| He's | the one. I saw | him. |
|---------|-----------------|-------|
| She's | | her. |
| It's | | it. |
| They're | the ones. I saw | them. |

| He's | the one I saw. |
|---------|------------------|
| She's | |
| It's | |
| They're | the ones I saw. |

Maple Street is in one of the older residential sections of Portstown. Look at the six stores.

One of them sells greeting cards and newspapers.
One of them fixes shoes.
One of them does dry cleaning.

One of them sells antiques.
One of them does photocopying.
One of them sells children's clothes.

## Exercise 1

*"Bygones" must be the one that sells antiques.*

Write five more sentences.

## Exercise 2

Antique store/copy shop/stationery store/dry cleaner's/children's boutique/shoe repair store

*A place that sells children's clothes is a children's boutique.*

Write five more sentences.

Look at these statements by the people who run (own or manage) the stores.

**Donald Kaufman** "I visit all the auctions, and I advertise in the local paper. It's a hobby as much as it is a business."

**Cheryl Madigan** "We bought the store when I retired. I like working with my husband, and it's nice to meet so many people."

**Vicky Calderon** "I have three children, and it was so hard to find nice clothes for them in Portstown. That's why I decided to start my own business."

**Penny Lee** "Actually, I'm not the owner; I'm just the manager. We do it all on the premises. If you bring in something at ten, it'll be ready by four."

**John Larue** "I used to teach typing and shorthand. So many offices have rotten equipment. The machines here are really expensive, but I lease them from the manufacturer."

**Tony Bianco** "I've been at this for 40 years. Of course the quality's gone down a lot…all these synthetic materials. If you ask me, leather's still the best."

*Cheryl Madigan must be the one that runs the stationery store.*
Write five more sentences on a separate sheet of paper.

*Cheryl Madigan is the woman who runs the place that sells greeting cards and newspapers.*

Write five more sentences on a separate sheet of paper.

Look at the statements in Exercise 3.

*Cheryl Madigan is the woman who bought a shop when she retired. She's the one who likes working with her husband.*

Write ten more sentences on a separate sheet of paper.

That's the club. I went to it last night. *That's the club I went to last night.*
Continue.

**1.** That's the hotel. I've often stayed in it. ...........................

**2.** This is the book. I've been reading it lately. ...................

**3.** She's the woman. I gave the documents to her. .............

**4.** Those are the girls. My sister teaches them. .................

**5.** These are the letters. You asked me to mail them. .........

**6.** He must be the boy. We saw him running away. ...........

**7.** This is the magazine. I told you about it. ........................

**8.** These must be the ones. You wanted me to find them.

That's the store. It sells antiques. *That's the store that sells antiques.*

That's the store. I was in it this morning. *That's the store I was in this morning.*

Continue.

**1.** She's the woman. I went to school with her. ..................

**2.** She's the woman. She went to school with me. .............

**3.** He's the man. He plays for the Dodgers. .......................

**4.** He's the man. I've seen him on TV a lot. .......................

**5.** They're the people. They live on my street. ...................

**6.** They're the people. I live near them. .............................

**7.** Those are the ones. I've been looking for them. ............

**8.** Those must be the ones. They were on my desk. ..........

# Unit 46

## Language Summary

*He went to California, WHERE he did this.*
*This is WHERE it happened.*

*The guard WHOSE cabin he was searching came in.*
*A beautiful woman, WHOSE hands were also tied, was lying beside him.*

Look at this ad from a New York newspaper.

## SEVEN-DAY BUS TOUR IN ENGLAND

### Kings Tours
### ITINERARY

**Day one** ·
**LONDON**
day: visit Tower of London & Buckingham Palace
evening: Jupiter Club—floor show
overnight: Upminster Hotel

**Day two**
**CAMBRIDGE**
day: go around colleges
evening: country pub—country dancing
overnight: University Arms Hotel

**Day three**
**STRATFORD-ON-AVON**
day: sightseeing
evening: theater visit—Romeo and Juliet
overnight: Falstaff Hotel

**Day four**
**OXFORD**
day: visit university
evening: Tudor Restaurant—special dinner
overnight: Hotel Academia

**Day five**
**NEW FOREST & BOURNEMOUTH**
day: see Winchester Cathedral
evening: Beaulieu National Motor Museum
overnight: Continental Hotel, Bournemouth

**Day six**
**BATH**
day: see Roman baths
evening: country pub—folksinging
overnight: Hotel Trajan

**Day seven**
**LONDON**
day: shopping West End
evening: National Theater—Hamlet
overnight: Airport Hotel

*Price includes breakfast and dinner*

SEE YOUR TRAVEL AGENT FOR DETAILS, OR CONTACT:

Kings Tours
1330 Broadway
New York, New York 10017
Tel: (212) 868-2222

## Exercise 1

The tour starts on Tuesday. The Kings Tours guide is telling a customer in the New York office about it.
Day 1
**A.** *On Tuesday we're going to be in London, where we'll visit the Tower of London and Buckingham Palace.*
**B.** *In the evening we're going to the Jupiter Club, where we'll see a floor show.*

Now write the schedule for Days 2, 3, 4, 5, 6, and 7.

## Exercise 2

The guide and the bus driver are discussing their last tour with American tourists and some of the things that happened.
Paul Biblowitz/passport was stolen in Cambridge.

**Driver:** *Do you remember Paul Biblowitz?*

**Guide:** *Yes, I do. He's the man whose passport was stolen in Cambridge.*
Write sentences with *whose*.

1. Martha Prior/husband danced on the table at the Jupiter Club.
2. The Rossis/little boy was sick on the bus in Oxford.
3. Kim Vaughn/suitcase broke on the first day.
4. Jim Gonzalez/wallet was stolen in London.
5. Bob Monski/wife got drunk in Bournemouth.
6. The MacDonalds/daughter got engaged to a waiter in Bath.

## Exercise 3

That's the club. Mr. Prior danced on the table there.

*That's the club where Mr. Prior danced on the table.*

He's the man. His wife didn't speak to him once during the tour.

*He's the man whose wife didn't speak to him once during the tour.*

Combine these sentences in the same way.

1. This is a picture of the Hotel Academia. We stayed there in Oxford.

2. Kim Vaughn was the woman. Her suitcase was full of bottles of medicine.

3. Bath was the place! Mr. MacDonald punched a waiter in the nose there.

4. This is a picture of Beaulieu. The National Motor Museum is located there.

5. Do you remember the Rossis? Their son got sick three times.

6. Bob Monski was the man. His wife drank a bottle and a half of wine.

7. Winchester Cathedral was the place. Paul Biblowitz broke his camera there.

8. She's the lady. Her husband was always late for the bus.

9. Mrs. MacDonald's the one. Her husband fell asleep during *Hamlet*.

10. Do you remember that pub near Cambridge? Jim Gonzalez sang some songs in Spanish there.

# Unit 47

## Language Summary

*This is the place WHERE it happened.*
*That's the day WHEN it happened.*
*He's the man WHO did it.*
*She's the one WHOSE friend did it.*

## Exercise 1

optometrist/tests people's eyes    *A person who tests people's eyes is an optometrist.*
bank/cash checks    *A place where you can cash checks is a bank.*
second Sunday in June/our fathers    *The second Sunday in June is the day when we remember our fathers.*
vacuum cleaner/cleans carpets    *A machine which cleans carpets is a vacuum cleaner.*
orphan/parents dead    *A child whose parents are dead is an orphan.*

Now write sentences from these cues.

1. lawn mower/cuts grass
   ................................................................

2. October 31/celebrate Halloween ................................

3. veterinarian/treats sick animals ................................

4. savings bank/borrow money to buy a house ................

5. widower/wife dead ................................................

6. camcorder/makes video recordings ..........................

7. reporter/writes for newspapers ................................

8. The Fourth of July/celebrate the birthday of the United
   States ................................................................

9. filling station/buy gas ............................................

10. VCR/records television programs ..........................

11. gym/do exercises ................................................

12. widow/husband dead ............................................

13. server/brings your food in a restaurant ..................

14. second Sunday in May/our mothers ......................

## Exercise 2

I gave the information to a woman.
She was sitting at the next desk.

*I gave the information to a woman who was sitting at the next desk.*

Continue.

1. I'll meet you at the coffee bar. You had cappuccino
   there yesterday. ................................................

2. Those are our neighbors. Their dog was just in a
   commercial on TV. ............................................

3. He had a party for the people. They worked for him
   during the campaign. ..........................................

4. Do you remember that day? We had a hurricane then.
   ................................................................

5. I saw you talking to a man. His hair was green.
   ................................................................

6. This is the letter. The customer complained about the
   service in the letter. ..........................................

7. There was a fire at the factory. He works there.
   ................................................................

8. She just finished reading the book. The teacher spoke
   about it last week. ............................................

9. I'll never forget the time. We saw the shooting star then.
   ................................................................

10. Here are the photos. We took them on our last vacation.
    ................................................................

# Unit 48

## Language Summary

*Alan Wolfe, who again escaped from the Maryland penitentiary, has been recaptured.*

*The construction industry, which is an important indicator of the economy's direction, reports fewer new buildings started in the last three months.*

*A recently found portrait, which experts refuse to attribute to Winslow Homer, was sold for a record $2 million by Northeby's.*

*Tim Miles, the racing driver whose legs were badly injured in last year's Grand Prix accident, says he will never race again.*

*Central Motors' Calypso, whose success has surprised CM officials as much as the competition, is now the best-selling car in the U.S.*

## Exercise 1

Study the **Language Summary** and then read the following article. The commas have been removed from the article. Replace them.

### ——— JFK Hijacking ———

A large shipment of silver bullion which is estimated to be worth $10,000,000 was hijacked in broad daylight yesterday from an armored truck. The truck which was en route to Kennedy Airport was waved to the side of the road by two men on the Van Wyck Expressway. The men who were armed were both dressed in police uniforms. The driver and the security guard who also had guns were asked to get out and show their identification. They were then attacked and overpowered by a number of men. They had been hiding in a stolen police van parked nearby.

Both vehicles then drove away. The security guards who they had tied up were taken with them. The armored truck was later found abandoned. The two guards whose hands were still tied were inside. The police uniforms which the thieves had rented from a theatrical supplier were on the front seat. The silver which was being transported from the Wall Street area to the airport was in kilo bars. The two guards whose injuries were not serious are being questioned by detectives.

## Exercise 2

George Steinmetz today fired Manager Willie Martin—again. (Steinmetz is the owner of the Los Angeles Strikers.)
*George Steinmetz, who is the owner of the Los Angeles Strikers, today fired Manager Willie Martin—again.*

Combine these sentences in the same way.

**1.** Bubba Caruthers broke his leg. (He plays for the Red Bay Canners.)

..................................................................

..................................................................

**2.** The new album by "The Tumbling Dice" has already sold one million copies. (It was recorded in Nashville.)

..................................................................

..................................................................

**3.** Dr. Lorraine Segal has won the Nobel Prize for science. (Barbara Watters interviewed her on TV last week.)

..................................................................

..................................................................

**4.** The racehorse Native Speaker was sold for $5 million yesterday. (Hector Ramirez rode it in the Kentucky Derby.)

..................................................................

..................................................................

**5.** William Paine will be the star of the new Hollywood movie Juke Box '58. (His last movie won an Academy Award.)

..................................................................

..................................................................

**6.** The rehabilitation center will be opened by the First Lady on Friday. (It has taken two years to build.) ....................

..................................................................

**7.** Natalia Sloservova is retiring from international tennis. (Komiko Sato beat her in the final at the U.S. Open.)

..................................................................

..................................................................

**8.** An antique table was auctioned for $40,000. (Chippenham made it in 1743.)

..................................................................

..................................................................

# Unit 49

## Language Summary

| to/for/from | which |
| on/in/about | whom |
| of/all of | |

**Defining relative clauses**
Formal, written style
*He was the man to whom I spoke.*

Spoken and informal written style
*He was the man* | *I spoke to.*
| *who I spoke to.*
| *that I spoke to.*

**Non-defining relative clauses**
Formal, written style
*Katherine Horton, with whom you spoke last November, is in charge of all conference logistics.*

Spoken and informal written style
*Katherine Horton, who you spoke with last November, is in charge of all conference logistics.*

### Exercise 1

Dorothy Daniels has just received this letter from the Sleeptight Bedding Company. Copy it out as a business letter with three paragraphs, capital letters, and correct punctuation.

sleeptight bedding company 115 down street gooseburg idaho 83651 october 15 1996 ms dorothy daniels 82 glendower road akron ohio 44313 dear ms daniels thank you for your recent order for a king-size comforter unfortunately we were unable to process your order because your check was written for the incorrect amount we are therefore returning your check as soon as we receive your check for $139.85 we will be happy to send you your comforter we appreciate your patronage and hope you will continue shopping at sleeptight sincerely rosemary loakes customer service representative

### Exercise 2

I took it back to the store I had bought it from.
*I took it back to the store from which I had bought it.*

Write these sentences in a more formal style.

1. Pat Henley is the secretary I spoke to on the telephone.
2. Continental Computers is the company she invested all her money in.
3. Preston is the Indiana town I saw a documentary about.
4. Wibalandia is a country I know nothing about.
5. The XL5000 is the microcomputer I paid $1,000 for.
6. Appletree Farm is the land we are going to build the new factory on.
7. You wrote to Ms. Judith Wall who I am replying for.
8. Helen Thomas is the woman who I got your address from.
9. Our Customer Service Department is the place questions should be sent to.
10. I am sure you wish to protect your company's good name, which you must be proud of.

### Exercise 3

We tried several garages. None of them had the parts in stock.
*We tried several garages, none of which had the parts in stock.*

Combine these sentences in the same way.

1. I spoke to two sales associates. One of them was extremely rude.
2. We bought two batteries. Neither of them worked.
3. We have employed many temporary secretaries from your agency. Most of them were reliable and efficient.
4. We have several vacation cottages. All of them are fully furnished.
5. There are over 20,000 regular Canners fans. Only a few of them misbehave at games.
6. There are eight candidates. Three of them are very well qualified.
7. We bought 2,000 light bulbs from your company. Many of them have since proved to be defective.
8. We spoke to two of your sales reps. Both of them refused to comment.
9. There are 600 students. The majority of them are Spanish speakers.
10. We received 30,000 roof tiles. About 10% of them were cracked on delivery.

### Exercise 4

Mrs. Jackson no longer works here. (You addressed the letter to her.)
*Mrs. Jackson, to whom you addressed the letter, no longer works here.*

Combine these sentences in the same way.

1. The bank counter was covered with black ink. (I had placed my new wallet on it.)
2. Harold Grant asked me to contact you. (I was speaking with him yesterday.)
3. Ms. Gloria Chan will provide a recommendation. (I was supervised by her at my last job.)
4. Walters-Reed Co. would like more information about your products. (We are acting for them as agents.)
5. The Calypso is still not available in this area. (We have been hearing a lot about it recently.)
6. The *Daily Post* advised me to contact the Better Business Bureau. (I saw your misleading advertisement in it.)

# Unit 50

## Language Summary

Relative clauses (review) introduced by *which, that, whose, who*

VACATION-BY-THE-SEA
**HOTEL GUIDE**

Rates shown are for one week (7 nights)
and include continental breakfast

**THOMAS TRAVEL**

| RATING | HOTEL | LOCATION | RATES |
|---|---|---|---|
| ★★ | APOLLO 60 rooms (30 ocean view) | Mykonos, Greece | $200 |
| ★★★ | AZTECA 300 rooms (200 with balcony) | Acapulco, Mexico | $220 |
| ★★★★ | BONAPARTE 120 rooms (all ocean view) | Biarritz, France | $250 |
| ★★★★★ | VASCO DA GAMA 212 rooms (90 ocean view) | Rio de Janeiro, Brazil | $300 |

## Exercise 1

Look at the sentences about the Apollo. Write similar ones about the Azteca.

The Apollo

1. *It's the one that's in Greece.*
2. *It's the one that's in Mykonos.*
3. *It's the only one that has two stars.*
4. *It's the one that costs $200.*
5. *The Apollo, which is in Greece, is a two-star hotel.*
6. *The Apollo, which is a two-star hotel, is in Mykonos.*
7. *The Apollo, which is in Mykonos, costs $200.*
8. *The Apollo, which costs $200, has two stars.*
9. *The Apollo has 60 rooms, 30 of which have an ocean view.*
10. *At the Apollo there will be guides who speak fluent Greek and English.*

## Exercise 2

Read this paragraph about the Bonaparte, and write a similar one about the Vasco da Gama.

The Bonaparte

*The Bonaparte, which overlooks the beach at Biarritz, is a four-star hotel. It is the only four-star hotel that we offer in this area. It has 120 rooms, all of which have an ocean view. The weekly rate is $250, which includes continental breakfast. At the hotel there will be guides who speak fluent French and English.*

**TOUR GROUP**
San Francisco      April 24-27

| Names | From | Native Language | Hotel |
|---|---|---|---|
| Teresa and Alberto Cruz | Monterrey, Mexico | Spanish | The Mark Hopkins |
| Sonia and Paulo Ferreira | Curitiba, Brazil | Portuguese | The St. Francis |
| Noriko and Ishiro Wada | Osaka, Japan | Japanese | The Four Seasons |
| Fatima and Ibrahim Nasser | Muscat, Oman | Arabic | The Fairmont |

## Exercise 3

1. Teresa and Alberto Cruz are the ones who come from Monterrey, Mexico.
2. Teresa and Alberto are the ones who speak Spanish.
3. Teresa Cruz, who's from Mexico, speaks Spanish.
4. Teresa and Alberto, who are from Mexico, are staying at the Mark Hopkins.
5. Alberto, whose native language is Spanish, is from Monterrey, Mexico.
6. Monterrey, which is in Mexico, is Teresa and Alberto's hometown.
7. Teresa, who's Mexican, is staying at the Mark Hopkins.
8. Alberto, whose wife is Teresa, is Mexican.
9. Teresa and Alberto are the ones who are staying at the Mark Hopkins.
10. Teresa, whose husband is Alberto, is from Mexico.

Make sentences about all the other tourists.

---

**PORTSTOWN DAILY ECHO,** Sept. 8
## COMMUNITY BULLETIN BOARD

A weekly feature of the "HOME" section in the Friday edition of the DAILY ECHO. Your ad of 16 words maximum plus your phone number costs only $5.00. Call 724-9600 to place your ad in next week's issue of the "HOME" section of the DAILY ECHO or mail in the coupon elsewhere on this page.

---

**BICYCLE** Raleigh Technium Olympian 21-spd bike, only slightly used. $250. 243-9186

**BRAND NEW** men's Wellington boots, size 11 1/2 B, Cordovan leather, never worn. $25. 243-7910

**CAFE CURTAINS** for kitchen, bath, den, diff. lengths, colors avail. Major retailer warehouse overstock, some imperf. 691-8000

**CAMERA** Kodak Instamatic, built-in flash. Used once. $25. 243-2362

**CAR RADIO** w/speakers, easy to install, Magnavox solid state, exc. cond.

$75. 243-5437

**CHEST OF DRAWERS** children's, 2 1/2 ft. hi, deep drawers, easy pull, painted wood w/Disney characters. $30. 691-8244

**COMPUTER** Orange PC, 486, 8MB RAM, 120MB HD, $400. 243-7910

**EXERCISE MACHINE** by Soloflex, including leg attachment & butterfly extension. Cost $1,300. Asking $780. 691-3845

**GOLF SET** Northwestern irons, 3 through 9 and sand wedge, 1, 3, & 5 wood. Asking $190. 620-9032

**IBM SELECTRIC** elec typewriter, self-correcting w/italic element plus standard, like new, must see. $250. 670-3480. Eves.

**KITCHEN SET,** chrome tubular legs, 46 in. x 28 in., white gold-flecked Formica top, 4 vinyl chairs, mint cond. $200. 243-2673

**PROWLERS BEWARE.** Guard dog on continuous loop cassette. Barks, growls, paces and no food to buy. $5. 243-6082

**ROLODEX** unused, phone/address file. Alphabet tab dividers, 500 blank cards 2 1/2 in. x 4 in. $5. 620-9693

**SPEAKERS** orig. pkg., never used. $150. 620-9778

**STROLLER** lt. wt. collapsible, sturdy construction, extra-hi handles, firm support for baby's back, good cond. $25. 691-3970

**TV B/W MOTOROLA,** portable, 13 in., exc. cond. No reasonable offer refused. 620-1565

**WEDDING GOWN** Elegant, long lace sleeves, sweetheart neck, beaded bodice. Size 8. Never worn. $300. 620-1354

---

## Exercise 1

Find abbreviations that mean:

1. black and white
2. high
3. excellent
4. original
5. speed
6. with
7. inches
8. lightweight
9. feet
10. available
11. package
12. electric
13. condition
14. evenings
15. imperfect

## Exercise 2

There are several expressions that mean "new" or "nearly new." What are they?

## Exercise 3

There are several expressions that describe the condition of the item. What are they?

## Exercise 4

1. List the items advertised that are used for recreation.

2. List the manufacturer's names in the ads.

## Exercise 5

Imagine that you want to sell one of your possessions. Fill out this form.

## SELLING THAT WHITE ELEPHANT?

**QUICK RESULTS IN THE WEEKLY "PENNY PINCHER" COMMUNITY BULLETIN BOARD**

Did you know that you can now advertise as many items as you wish—
**FOR ONLY $10.00**

Every Friday in the DAILY ECHO
Portstown's biggest newspaper!
Just fill out the coupon with not more than 16 words plus your phone number

✂·············YOUR BARGAIN COUPON···················

Name..........................  Phone........................
Address.......................  Money Order ☐
...........Zip..........  Check ☐

## Exercise 6

Now write four similar ads for four more of your possessions on another sheet of paper.

## Exercise 7

Describing things in an ad is different from descriptions in a more formal text. Look at the table in Unit 51 of the Student Book.

He has a .............. car. (French, old, rusty, dirty)
*He has a dirty, old, rusty French car.*
Rewrite these sentences, putting the adjectives in the most appropriate order.

1. It's a .............. painting. (landscape, valuable, 19th century)

2. She lives in a .............. apartment. (three-bedroom, spacious, penthouse)

3. I just bought a .............. briefcase. (leather, brown, terrific)

4. I'd like .............. eggs. (dozen, two, fresh, brown, large)

5. He has an .............. camcorder. (brand-new, expensive, palm-sized)

6. Look at those .............. vases. (antique, porcelain, Japanese)

7. I'm looking for a ............. sweater. (V-neck, green, washable, wool)

8. I was bitten by a ..............dog. (black, huge, Rottweiler, savage)

9. She drives a .............. convertible. (yellow, Plymouth, light, little, cute)

# Unit 52

*Charles Orson*

1. Terry Gallagher
2. Beth Yakamura
3. Jean Emery
4. Wally Cowan
5. Joey Maida
6. Monica Briscoe
7. Dick Harris
8. Sheena Gray
9. Elizabeth Marrero
10. David Cheung
11. Roland Prendergast
12. Doreen Barker

## Exercise 1

**A:** *Who's the short, heavy man with glasses?*
**B:** *That's Charles Orson.*

Continue.

1. **A:** ...................................................................
   **B:** ...................................................................

2. **A:** ...................................................................
   **B:** ...................................................................

3. **A:** ...................................................................
   **B:** ...................................................................

4. **A:** ...................................................................
   **B:** ...................................................................

5. **A:** ...................................................................
   **B:** ...................................................................

6. **A:** ...................................................................
   **B:** ...................................................................

7. **A:** ...................................................................
   **B:** ...................................................................

8. **A:** ...................................................................
   **B:** ...................................................................

9. **A:** ...................................................................
   **B:** ...................................................................

10. **A:** ...................................................................
    **B:** ...................................................................

11. **A:** ...................................................................
    **B:** ...................................................................

12. **A:** ...................................................................
    **B:** ...................................................................

## Exercise 2

Write a short description of one of your classmates. Read it aloud. See if the other students can guess who it is.

Look at the example and complete the table.

| *the man who has long hair* | *the man with long hair* | *the long-haired man* |
| --- | --- | --- |
| the woman who has blue eyes | ................................................... ................................................... | ................................................... ................................................... |
| ................................................... ................................................... | the woman with gray hair | ................................................... ................................................... |
| ................................................... ................................................... | ................................................... ................................................... | the bearded man |
| the woman who has thin lips | ................................................... ................................................... | ................................................... ................................................... |

Write brief descriptions of these people.

**1.**

**2.**

**3.**

**4.**

**5.**

**6.**

# Unit 53

## Language Summary

*He (did this) to (do that).*
*He sent (someone) to (do that).*

*He (did this) in order to (do that).*
*In order to* | *(do that), he (did this).*
*To* |

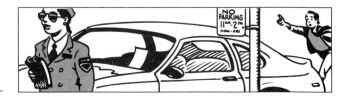

### A hard luck story

Hodges had a bad day. His car broke down, and he was in a no-parking zone. So he went into a store to borrow a pen and paper to leave a note for the traffic police. The pen, however, was like his car. It didn't work. He decided to go back to the store to buy a pen, but he found another little problem. He only had a $100 bill and the salesclerk couldn't change it. So he went off to find a bank to change the bill to buy the pen to write on the paper to put on his car to tell the traffic police that his car had broken down.

As he left the bank he spotted a phone booth. He tried to call a garage to send a truck to tow the car away, but the number was busy. When he got back to his car he found a parking ticket on the windshield. The story has, however, a happy ending. The driver wrote to the Police Commissioner to explain what had happened. The police officer who read the letter decided to let him off the $25 parking fine. She said that even if the man's story was not true, it was so clever he deserved to be let off!

1. Why did he want to borrow a pen and paper?
2. Why did he decide to go back to the store?
3. Why did he go to find a bank?
4. Why did he want to leave a note on the car?
5. Why did he want the garage to send a truck?
6. Why did he write to the Police Commissioner?

### Exercise 1

Why did he go into a store?

**A.** *He went into a store to borrow a pen.*
**B.** *He went into a store in order to borrow a pen.*

Write two answers to each of the questions.

### Exercise 2

She hired a secretary { *to answer the phone.*
*to help with her work.*
*to type her letters.*

Complete these.

1. He called a plumber ....................................................................................................................................

2. She called an electrician ..............................................................................................................................

3. I called a mechanic .......................................................................................................................................

4. They commissioned an artist ........................................................................................................................

5. We went to a photographer ...........................................................................................................................

6. She sent him to the optician .........................................................................................................................

7. They called the waiter over ...........................................................................................................................

8. She went to a specialist ................................................................................................................................

9. Mrs. Worthington hired a bodyguard ............................................................................................................

10. He bought a mean dog .................................................................................................................................

### Exercise 3

Now complete these.

1. He boiled some water ....................................................................................................................................

2. He smashed the window .................................................................................................................................

3. She bought a paper .......................................................................................................................................

4. She used a credit card ...................................................................................................................................

5. I picked up the receiver ..................................................................................................................................

6. He took some aspirin ......................................................................................................................................

# Unit 54

## Language Summary

| I (did this) | so that | he | could / couldn't | (do that). | or | So that | he | could / couldn't | (do that) | I (did this). |
|---|---|---|---|---|---|---|---|---|---|---|
| | | this | would / wouldn't | (happen). | | | this | would / wouldn't | (happen) | |
| I (do this) ('m doing this) | | she | can / can't | (do that). | | | she | can / can't | (do that) | I (do this). |
| | | this | will / won't | (happen). | | | this | will / won't | (happen) | I'm (doing that). |

When 006 returned from the Indian Ocean, a new car was waiting for him.
It looked like an ordinary production model but it had a number of extra features.

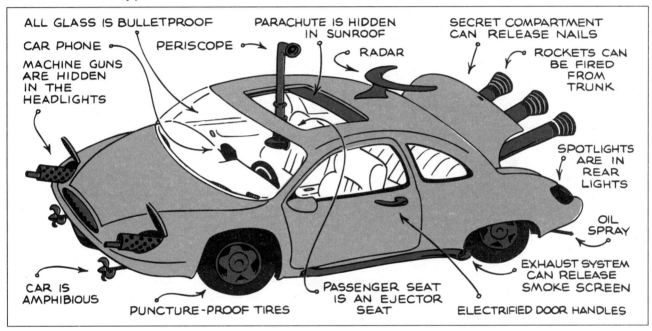

ALL GLASS IS BULLETPROOF
CAR PHONE
PERISCOPE
MACHINE GUNS ARE HIDDEN IN THE HEADLIGHTS
PARACHUTE IS HIDDEN IN SUNROOF
RADAR
SECRET COMPARTMENT CAN RELEASE NAILS
ROCKETS CAN BE FIRED FROM TRUNK
SPOTLIGHTS ARE IN REAR LIGHTS
OIL SPRAY
CAR IS AMPHIBIOUS
PUNCTURE-PROOF TIRES
PASSENGER SEAT IS AN EJECTOR SEAT
EXHAUST SYSTEM CAN RELEASE SMOKE SCREEN
ELECTRIFIED DOOR HANDLES

### Exercise 1

*There's a periscope so that the car can operate as a submarine.*

Why do you think the other optional features have been put on the car? Write eleven sentences with *so that*.

### Exercise 3

006 did several things before his next mission.
He grew a beard. Why?

*So that no one would recognize him.*
or *So that he could take on another identity.*
or *So that he would look different.*

Continue.

**1.** He bought several bathing suits. Why? ...........................

...............................................................................

**2.** He took tennis lessons. Why? .......................................

...............................................................................

**3.** He studied Italian. Why? .............................................

...............................................................................

### Exercise 2

*006 was given a false tooth with poison in it, so that he could kill himself if he was captured.*

What other things do you think he might have been given for his mission and why? Write three more sentences.

**4.** He began running 20 miles a week. Why? .....................

...............................................................................

**5.** He got a passport under the name Roger Moore. Why?

...............................................................................

**6.** He learned to repair boats. Why? .................................

...............................................................................

**7.** He visited Greece. Why? .............................................

...............................................................................

**8.** He learned to fly a helicopter. Why? .............................

...............................................................................

# Unit 55

## Language Summary

| Do this | so that you don't<br>in order not to | do that. | |
| --- | --- | --- | --- |
| | to<br>so that you can | avoid | that.<br>doing that. |
| | in order to<br>to | prevent<br>stop | that (from happening).<br>something from happening.<br>keep somebody from doing that. |

---

### How to Prevent Jet Lag

**BEFORE YOUR TRIP:**
- Stay on a sensible schedule.
- Don't deprive yourself of sleep.
- Don't eat foods that are heavy or difficult to digest.

**DURING YOUR FLIGHT:**
- Drink plenty of fluids.
- Avoid alcoholic beverages.
- Eat only when you are hungry (which is not necessarily when the flight attendant serves your food).
- Don't go to sleep on the plane, but sit with your eyes closed and relax.

**ONCE YOU ARRIVE:**
- Socialize.
- Start adapting to your new environment—the language and culture—as soon as you arrive.

- Don't nap.
- Stay out-of-doors. If you've traveled east, be outdoors in the morning; if you've traveled west, be outdoors in the afternoon.
- Exercise.

---

### Exercise 1

*Before your trip, get enough sleep so that you don't get jet lag.*

Write two other things to do before your trip, four things to do during your flight, and five things to do once you arrive in order to prevent jet lag.

---

### How to Prevent Motion Sickness

In general:
- Get enough sleep before you travel.
- Have a light, easy-to-digest meal an hour before you leave.
- Don't have alcoholic beverages right before or during the trip.
- Take over-the-counter motion-sickness medicine (but be aware of their possible side effects—drowsiness, dry mouth, and blurry vision).
- Or eat candied ginger (which doesn't have any adverse side effects) or take ginger root capsules.
- Sit still, but don't try to read.

If you're in a car:
- Sit in the front of the vehicle, but not over the wheels.
- Keep the window open.
- Keep your head forward, and concentrate on the horizon.

If you're on a boat:
- Stand on deck, not below deck.
- Get a cabin in the middle of the ship, where the least amount of rolling is felt.
- Focus on a stationary point in the sky or on land in the distance.

---

### Exercise 2

*Get enough sleep before you travel to avoid motion sickness.*

Write five other things to do to avoid motion sickness.

### Exercise 3

*If you're in a car, sit in the front of the vehicle but not over the wheels to keep from getting motion sickness.*

Write two other things to keep from getting motion sickness in a car.

### Exercise 4

*If you're on a boat, stand on deck, not below deck, in order to avoid getting motion sickness.*

Write two other things to keep from getting motion sickness on a boat.

# Unit 56

## Language Summary

*The house was SO beautiful THAT they bought it.*

*She had SO | much work | THAT she couldn't sleep at night.*
*             | many problems |*

*They worked SO hard THAT they hardly ever saw each other.*

*It was SUCH a beautiful house THAT they bought it.*

*He had SUCH a lot of | work | THAT he couldn't sleep at night.*
*                  | problems |*

---

## Exercise 1

**1. A.** *The music was so wonderful that I went right out and bought the CD.*
**B.** *It was such wonderful music that I went right out and bought the CD.*

Look at the example and transform the sentences from the reviews in the same way.

**2. A.**.................................................................

**B.**.................................................................

**3. A.**.................................................................

**B.**.................................................................

**4. A.**.................................................................

**B.**.................................................................

**5. A.**.................................................................

**B.**.................................................................

### ★★ Broadway's latest hit musical ★★

# DESTINATION HAPPINESS

Grand Theater • 8 p.m. daily • Matinee 3 p.m., • Wed. and Sat.

"Very, very, good. It will run for years."
N.Y. DOINGS

"Spectacular dancing. I enjoyed every minute!"
ENTERTAINMENT P.M.

"Kitty Millici sang brilliantly. She will become a superstar!"
WMBS-TV

"A most entertaining show. The whole family will enjoy it"
WHIT-RADIO

"Wonderful music. I went right out and bought the CD." DAILY POST

Write similar sentences about "Sudden Departure" and "The Wrong Connection."

### Have you read P.D. Jameson's new thriller?

# SUDDEN DEPARTURE

Pantab books $24.95

"A tense, gripping thriller. It will sell millions."
DAILY POST

"A winner! Terrifying. I couldn't sleep for a week."
CARL STEPHENS

"Absolutely fascinating. I couldn't put it down."
CITY TIMES

"Believable story of the near future. Everyone should read it!"
PUBLISHERS MONTHLY

"Exciting plot. It would make a wonderful movie." ENTERTAINMENT P.M.

### Charles Olson's newest hit movie:

# The Wrong Connection

## Now playing:

• ABC Cinema 2    • Bayview Twin 1
• ABC Midway    • Galleria North Sixplex

"Hilarious. I couldn't stop laughing." –WEEK IN REVIEW

"Funny and touching. I didn't know whether to laugh or cry."
–GENE SHALLOW, TODAY (WBS-TV)

"Highly entertaining. The audience was shrieking with laughter."
–VIEWS AND PREVIEWS

"Valerie Robeson is very talented. She deserves an Academy Award." –BAYVIEW NEWS

"Tremendously amusing. It's sure to become a comedy classic."
–NOW WEEKLY

## Exercise 2

Write a short review of a book you have read or a movie or play you have seen recently.

# Unit 57

## Language Summary

*There was a lounge | which had a dance floor.*
*| with a dance floor.*

*They heard him. He was screaming.*
*They heard him screaming.*

*many of whom/some of whom/half of whom/thirteen of whom*

---

### METROPOLIS REALTY
3538 Brunswick Avenue, Kendall Park, NJ 08824 (201) 297-0200

**ML #76926    Address: 118 Longhill Road, Princeton**

**Description:** Six-year-old, two-story, Colonial-style dwelling on 6 acres of densely wooded land. Wall-to-wall carpet except kitchen; thermoplane windows.
Basement: Full; oil-burning furnace

**First floor:**
Entrance foyer: 10' x 3'
Kitchen: 10' x 11', built-in dishwasher and microwave oven
Dining area: 15' x 10', cathedral ceiling
Living room: 21' x 16', floor-to-ceiling stone fireplace
Master bedroom: 16' x 11', bath with whirlpool tub

**Second floor:**
Loft bedroom/den: 16' x 16'
Bedroom: 15' x 14'
Bath with stall shower

**Remarks:** Twenty-mile view from back porch
**Price:** $310,000

---

### Exercise 1

**A.** *There's a back porch which has a twenty-mile view.*
**B.** *There's a back porch with a twenty-mile view.*

Write four more sentences of each type.

**1. A.**...............................................................
...............................................................
**B.**...............................................................
...............................................................

**2. A.**...............................................................
...............................................................
**B.**...............................................................
...............................................................

**3. A.**...............................................................
...............................................................
**B.**...............................................................
...............................................................

**4. A.**...............................................................
...............................................................
**B.**...............................................................
...............................................................

---

### Exercise 2

There are about two hundred and fifty million people in the United States, of whom many are immigrants, that is, they were born outside the United States. These immigrants, some of whom arrived in the 1980s, have come from all over the world. Look at the chart below.

**The New Americans**
**Immigrants, by Country of Birth, 1981–1990**

| | |
|---|---|
| 1,653,000 | Mexico |
| 495,300 | Phillipines |
| 401,400 | Vietnam |
| 388,800 | China (PRC and Taiwan) |
| 338,800 | Korea |
| 251,800 | Dominican Republic |
| 261,900 | India |
| 214,600 | El Salvador |
| 213,800 | Jamaica |
| 159,200 | Cuba |
| 154,800 | Iran |
| 145,600 | Laos |
| 142,100 | the United Kingdom |
| 140,200 | Haiti |
| 124,400 | Colombia |
| 119,200 | Canada |
| 116,600 | Cambodia |
| 97,400 | Poland |
| 84,000 | former Soviet Union |
| 70,100 | Germany |

*Millions of immigrants arrived in the 1980s, just under 500,000 of whom came from the Philippines.*

100,000 200,000 300,000 400,000 500,000 600,000 700,000 800,000 900,000 1,000,000 1,500,000 2,000,000

Write eleven sentences like this, using: just over 400,000/more than 1,650,000/just under 160,000/about 140,000/approximately 97,000/almost 215,000/well over 380,000/just over 250,000/around 119,000/about 338,000/just over 70,000.

---

### Exercise 3

Sheila Yarnell appears on television variety shows. She impersonates famous people. She is often asked how she manages to do it.

She videotapes them when they are performing on television.
*She videotapes them performing on television.*

Continue.

**1.** She listens to them as they are speaking.

................................................................

**2.** She takes pictures of them when they are smiling and frowning.

................................................................

**3.** She imitates politicians when they are giving speeches.

................................................................

**4.** She watches popular singers every time they appear on TV.

................................................................

# Unit 58

## Language Summary

*It was raining. She took her umbrella.*

*She took her umbrella BECAUSE it was raining.*

*It wasn't raining. He took his umbrella.*

| ALTHOUGH THOUGH EVEN THOUGH | *it wasn't raining, he took his umbrella.* |

---

### Exercise 1

Fill in the blanks with *because* or *although*.

1. She applied for the job as personnel manager ................... she liked meeting people.

2. She got good grades on her exams ................... she never seemed to do much work.

3. ................... he is very well-off, he drives a cheap second-hand car.

4. The union was offered a good raise in pay ................... production had increased by 20%.

5. I'm going to buy the new album by The Tumbling Dice ................... they're my favorite group.

6. Her car refused to start ................... she had just had it tuned up.

### Exercise 2

He was depressed.   (He managed to smile.)
                   (He stopped seeing his friends.)

*He managed to smile although he was depressed.*
*He stopped seeing his friends because he was depressed.*

Write two sentences for each of the following.

1. She is handicapped.   (She needed a special car.)
                      (She took part in the marathon.)

2. They're very religious.   (They never go to church.)
                      (They go to church every Sunday.)

3. He fell 300 feet.   (He was killed.)
                (He didn't hurt himself.)

4. The room was stuffy.   (She opened the window.)
                     (She didn't open the window.)

5. The program was entertaining.   (He turned it off.)
                         (He watched it to the end.)

6. The ring was valuable.   (She threw it into the river.)
                    (She kept it in a safe deposit box.)

7. The service had been excellent.   (She left a big tip.)
                         (She didn't leave a tip.)

8. He was furious.   (He didn't say a word.)
                (He shouted.)

### Exercise 3

Even though he wrote three letters, he didn't get a reply.
*He wrote three letters, but he didn't get a reply.*

Rewrite these sentences in the same way.

1. They lost, although they played very well.

2. Though they thought the exam had been easy, they all failed.

3. Even though she smoked, drank, and never got any exercise, she lived to be 100.

4. The police couldn't prove anything although they knew she was guilty.

5. He didn't get the job even though everyone thought he was the best person for it.

### Exercise 4

Betty Harmon, Vice-President of Marketing for WE 'R' TOYS, interviewed several applicants for the job below. She made notes on each one. Look at the notes that she made on Richard Andrews.

**WE 'R' TOYS INC.**
Manufacturers of quality toys since 1958

We are looking for a dynamic marketing executive to join our highly successful sales team in the Northeast. The ideal candidate will be highly qualified with a proven track record in marketing and will be familiar with N.Y. and New England states. The successful candidate will be based in New York but will travel extensively in the Northeast. Master's degree in business a plus. Excellent salary and benefits.

SEND RESUME TO:
**V-P Marketing, WE 'R' TOYS INC., Eastwood Industrial Park, Dearborn, Michigan 48126**

Richard Andrews

| PROS | CONS |
|---|---|
| some marketing experience | no experience in the toy industry |
| ambitious | has never stayed long in one job |
| referred by Jack Flournoy | no master's degree in business |
| prepared to travel | is getting married next month |
| very familiar with New York | doesn't know the rest of Northeast |
| well-dressed | needed a haircut |
| made good eye contact | weak handshake |

*Although he has some marketing experience, he has no experience in the toy industry.*

Write six sentences with *although*.

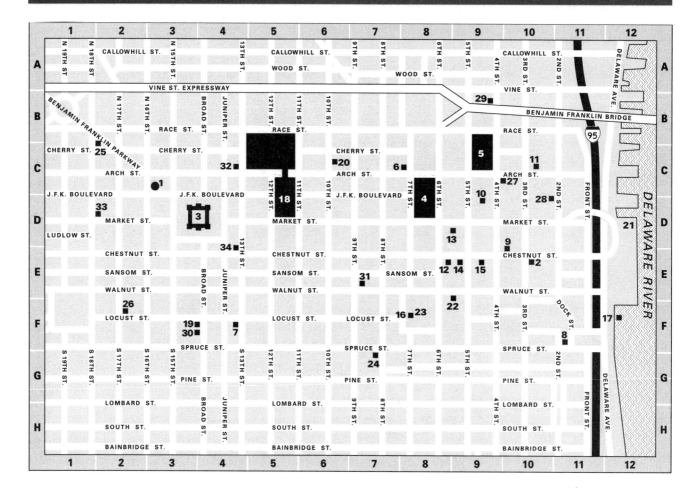

# Philadelphia: CENTER CITY

## TOURIST CENTERS

**1.** (C-3) Philadelphia Visitor's Center, 1525 JFK Boulevard (215-636-3300).

**2.** (E-10) Independence National Historical Park Visitors Center, 3rd & Chestnut Sts. (215-636-1666).

## PUBLIC BUILDINGS

**3.** (D-3, 4) City Hall, Broad & Market Sts. Largest city hall in the U.S.

**4.** (C-8) U.S. Court House, 6th & Market Sts.

**5.** (C-9) U.S. Mint, 5th & Arch Sts. Largest mint in the U.S.

## MUSEUMS

**6.** (C-7, 8) Afro-American Historical and Cultural Museum, 7th & Arch Sts. A showcase for African-American culture and heritage. Closed Mondays.

**7.** (F-4) Historical Society of Pennsylvania, 1300 Locust St. Vast collection of paintings, artifacts, documents, and research material from pre-Revolutionary War to 1850.

**8.** (F-11) "Man Full of Trouble" Tavern Museum, 125 Spruce St. Only 18th century tavern standing in Philadelphia.

**9.** (E-10) Philadelphia Maritime Museum, 321 Chestnut St. Nautical exhibits plus Philadelphia's maritime history.

**10.** (D-9) National Museum of American Jewish History, 5th St. above Market St. The American Jewish experience from 1654 to the present.

## HISTORICAL SITES

**11.** (C-10) Betsy Ross House, 234 Arch St. Home of the woman who made first American flag.

**12.** (E-8, 9) Independence Hall, Chestnut St. between 5th & 6th Sts. Nation's most significant shrine. Declaration of Independence adopted here, July 4, 1776; U.S. Constitution ratified here.

**13.** (D-8, 9) Liberty Bell Pavilion Market, between 5th & 6th Sts. In new pavilion, visitors can touch famed Bell.

**14.** (E-9) Old City Hall, 5th & Chestnut Sts. Where Supreme Court met, 1790-1800. Exhibition on colonial life.

**15.** (E-9) Second Bank of the U.S., Chestnut betw. 4th & 5th Sts. Restored as Portrait Gallery of History, featuring works from 1740-1840.

**16.** (F-8) Tomb of the Unknown Soldier of the American Revolution, Washington Square.

**17.** (F-12) U.S.S. Olympia, Penn's Landing. Commodore Dewey's flagship during the Battle of Manila Bay in the Spanish-American war.

## PLACES OF INTEREST

**18.** (D-5) Reading Terminal Market, betw. 11th & 12th Sts. Once the hub of the railroad, now part of the Pennsylvania Convention Center.

**19.** (F-3, 4) Academy of Music, Broad & Locust Sts.

**20.** (C-6) Chinese Cultural Community Center, 125 N. 10th St. Mandarin design building.

**21.** (D-12) Penn's Landing, Delaware Ave. from Race to Lombard. Fascinating sights including exhibits, ships, and special events.

**22.** (F-8, 9) Penn Mutual Observation Deck, 6th & Walnut Sts.

**23.** (F-8) Washington Square, Walnut St. betw. 6th & 7th Sts.

## HOSPITAL

**24.** (G-7) Pennsylvania Hospital, 8th & Spruce Sts.

## HOTELS

**25.** (C-1, 2) Four Seasons, 18th & The Parkway.

**26.** (F-2) Warwick Hotel, 17th & Locust Sts.

## PLACES OF WORSHIP

**27.** (C-9, 10) Friends Meeting House, 4th & Arch Sts.

**28.** (D-10, 11) Christ Church, 2nd St. north of Market St. Nation's founders worshipped here. Episcopal.

**29.** (B-9) St. Augustine's Roman Catholic Church, 4th St. above Race St.

## THEATERS

**30.** (F-3, 4) Merrian Theater, 250 S. Broad St.

**31.** (E-7) Walnut Street Theater, 9th & Walnut Sts.

## BUS TERMINALS

**32.** (C-4) Trailways, 13th & Arch Sts.

**33.** (D-1, 2) Greyhound, 18th & Market Sts.

## DEPARTMENT STORES

**34.** (D-4) John Wanamaker, 13th betw. Market & Chestnut Sts.

Trace the following directions on the map.

Walk out of the Philadelphia Visitor's Center (JFK Blvd. and North 16th Street) and turn left. Make the first right onto 15th Street. Continue on 15th Street for three blocks to Chestnut Street. Go left on Chestnut Street, past City Hall for ten blocks. Turn right at 6th Street and walk into the park.

Where are you? ....................................................................................................................................

What buildings can you see in the park? ...................................................................................................

**Exercise 2**

Write directions from the Tomb of the Unknown Soldier to the U.S. Mint.

Write directions from the U.S. Mint to the Academy of Music.

**Exercise 3**

In Philadelphia, where would you go to:

**1.** hear a symphony concert? ...........................................
...........................................................................

**2.** see an exhibition about ships? ...................................
...........................................................................

**3.** see the Delaware River? ............................................
...........................................................................

**4.** hear a symphony orchestra? .......................................
...........................................................................

**5.** appear as a witness at a trial? ...................................
...........................................................................

**6.** see money being made? ...........................................
...........................................................................

**7.** see a play? ...........................................................
...........................................................................

**8.** get a good view of Philadelphia? ................................
...........................................................................

**9.** catch a bus to New York? ..........................................
...........................................................................

**10.** see where the Declaration of Independence was signed?
...........................................................................

**Exercise 4**

Why couldn't you:

**1.** visit the Afro-American Historical and Cultural Museum

   on Monday afternoon? .....................................................

   ...................................................................................

**2.** get money at the Second Bank of the U.S.? ....................

   ...................................................................................

**3.** stand on the corner of Market and Broad Streets? ..........

   ...................................................................................

**4.** shake hands with Betsy Ross? .......................................

   ...................................................................................

**5.** catch a train at Reading Terminal? ................................

   ...................................................................................

**Exercise 5**

Now write directions from your home to your school.

# Unit 60

## Language Summary

It was snowing, so they canceled the game.　　or　They canceled the game | because it was　snowing.
　　　　　　　　　　　　　　　　　　　　　　　　　　　　　　　| because of the　snow.

　　　　　　　　　　　　　　　　　　　　　　or　Because it was snowing, | they canceled the game.
　　　　　　　　　　　　　　　　　　　　　　　　Because of the snow,　|

It was snowing, but they didn't cancel the game.　or　They didn't cancel the game | although | it was snowing.
　　　　　　　　　　　　　　　　　　　　　　　　　　　　　　　　　　| in spite of | the snow.
　　　　　　　　　　　　　　　　　　　　　　　　　　　　　　　　　　| despite |

　　　　　　　　　　　　　　　　　　　　　　or　Although it | was snowing, | they didn't cancel the game.
　　　　　　　　　　　　　　　　　　　　　　　　In spite of | the snow, |
　　　　　　　　　　　　　　　　　　　　　　　　Despite |

It was hard, but she managed to win.　　　　or　It was hard. | However, | she managed to win.
　　　　　　　　　　　　　　　　　　　　　　　　　　　　　| Nevertheless, |

　　　　　　　　　　　　　　　　　　　　　　or　It was hard. She managed to win, | however.
　　　　　　　　　　　　　　　　　　　　　　　　　　　　　　　　　　　| nevertheless.

　　　　　　　　　　　　　　　　　　　　　　or　It was hard. She managed, | however, | to win.
　　　　　　　　　　　　　　　　　　　　　　　　　　　　　　　　| nevertheless, |

## Exercise

Read the following news items and fill in the blanks with: because/because of/although/in spite of/nevertheless.

In Mandanga, John Curtis, the kidnapped American business-person, was released today _____ no ransom had been paid. He was found in a bus shelter in the early hours of this morning with his hands and feet tied. _____ his terrible experience, he was well and cheerful, _____ he was tired and hungry. The Mandangan police had refused to allow the family members to pay the ransom, _____ they had tried on several occasions. It is thought the kidnappers released Mr. Curtis after an appeal on television by his wife.

Orange Computers announced this afternoon that it has just won a $450 million order _____ fierce international competition. _____ the order, placed by the government of Wibalandia, the jobs of 80 employees at the Austin, Texas plant, which had been threatened _____ falling orders, will now be saved. _____ the economic recession continues to worsen, the company is optimistic that more orders will be placed for its new NZ series of computers. _____, the company states that its California plant will still have to close with the loss of 120 jobs.

The New Jersey Turnpike was closed for four hours today _____ a multiple crash involving hundreds of vehicles. At one point, visibility was down to 20 feet in some places _____ thick fog, and the road surface was treacherous _____ there were patches of ice. Drivers continued to go too fast _____ police warnings. _____ this "highway madness" and the terrible weather conditions, the police decided to close the turnpike. The police advise drivers not to drive unless it is absolutely necessary.

A 14-month-old baby miraculously escaped death this afternoon. _____ a 60-foot fall from a 5th story balcony, 14-month-old Steven Paine survived unhurt. Steven had somehow managed to crawl over the balcony railing. _____ he landed on concrete, he didn't even cry and was picked up by a neighbor and rushed to the hospital. After an examination, Steven was able to return home with nothing worse than minor bruises.

An estimated 20,000 people turned out to greet the president in Portstown today _____ terrible weather conditions. _____ nuclear protesters had threatened to disrupt the visit, their shouts of protest were drowned by the cheering crowds. _____ the visit, schoolchildren had been let out of school early and the president's route was lined with flag-waving children. Local police had mounted their tightest security operation ever. _____, the president managed to break free from his bodyguards and mingled with the crowd, chatting and shaking hands.

# Unit 61

## Exercise 1

Find words in the text that mean:

**1.** look into a matter

**2.** restrain by using greater strength

**3.** injure, using fingernails

**4.** took away a weapon

**5.** someone who looks after a building

**6.** exceeding what is reasonable

## Exercise 2

They overpowered the woman. Then they charged her with armed robbery.

*After overpowering the woman, they charged her with armed robbery.*

**1.** She refused to pay the fare. Then she hit the driver.

........................................................................

**2.** She hit the driver. Then she fought the police who came to his aid.

........................................................................

**3.** She arrived at home. Then she had a big shot of gin.

........................................................................

---

**DAILY ECHO**, MONDAY, DECEMBER 1

## Englishwoman, 93, Attacks Cabbie with Cane

LONDON, NOV. 30–A 93-year-old woman was jailed here for a night on a charge of armed robbery after she refused to pay what she considered an exorbitant taxi fare, then hit the driver with her walking cane and fought police who came to his aid.

Clarissa Baines refused to pay the £20 (about $32) fare on Friday. When the taxi driver protested, she hit him with her cane.

When the security guards at the apartment building where she lives came to his aid, she attacked them too. Two police officers who came to investigate were kicked, scratched, and hit with the cane.

After finally overpowering the woman, they charged her with armed robbery and resisting arrest, "disarmed" her, and took her off to jail.

Back at home, she was reported to have recovered with the aid of a big shot of gin.

---

**DAILY ECHO**, WEDNESDAY, NOVEMBER 5

## Piranha Bites a Baby's Hand

MIDDLEBURG, NOV. 4—A family's pet piranha fish was up for sale last night after it took a bite at their baby daughter.

The 15-inch long, flesh-eating fish named "Jaws" jumped clear of its tank and bit Katherine Pelli's finger as she trailed her hand near the water.

Her horrified mother Margaret, 26, said, "I was shaking with fear afterwards. I just want it out of the house."

Mrs. Pelli's 30-year-old husband Frank, who breeds tropical fish as a hobby, bought the fish 10 months ago for $50.

After the attack, 17-month-old Katherine was left with a badly cut finger. The fish simply dropped back into its tank which stands in the family's living room at their home on Hoyt Street in the Fair Meadows section of this city.

## Exercise 3

Read the passage and complete these sentences in your own words.

**1.** The fish was so dangerous that ...........................................................

**2.** It bit her finger while she was ...........................................................

**3.** Her mother was so terrified that ...........................................................

**4.** Frank's hobby is ...........................................................

**5.** The piranha's teeth were so sharp that ...........................................................

**6.** The fish was kept in ...........................................................

## Exercise 4

A man who is 40 years old is a 40-year-old man.

Continue.

**1.** A contract that is worth 15 million dollars is ...........................................

**2.** A suit that cost 200 dollars is ...........................................

**3.** A journey that takes 2 hours is ...........................................

**4.** A working week of 38 hours is ...........................................

**5.** A lesson of 50 minutes is ...........................................

**6.** A fish that is 15 inches long is ...........................................

**7.** A bag of potatoes that weighs 10 pounds is ...........................................

**8.** A tank that holds 20 gallons is ...........................................

# Unit 62

## Language Summary

*I don't know WHAT to do.*
*WHAT I saw surprised me.*
*That's not WHAT we're here for.*

### Exercise 1

What should I do?
*I don't know what to do.*
Rewrite these sentences in the same way.

**1.** What should I order for lunch? ......................................

..............................................................................

**2.** What should I do about my toothache? .........................

..............................................................................

**3.** What should I say to my boss? ....................................

..............................................................................

**4.** What should I get my nephew for his birthday? .............

..............................................................................

**5.** What should I say in the letter? ...................................

..............................................................................

**6.** What should I put on the form? ....................................

..............................................................................

### Exercise 2

I'll tell you everything I can. *I'll tell you what I can.*

Rewrite these sentences in the same way.

**1.** She answered all the questions she could.

**2.** He gave them all the money they needed.

**3.** They told him everything they knew.

**4.** She packed all the things she could.

**5.** They didn't have the things I wanted.

**6.** He spent all the money he had saved.

**7.** She noted all the information that was necessary.

**8.** She translated all the words she could.

**9.** They wrote down all the things they remembered.

**10.** He stole all the things he needed to stay alive.

### Exercise 3

I saw something that surprised me. *What I saw surprised me.*

Rewrite these sentences in the same way.

**1.** He said something that offended a lot of people.

**2.** He ate something that made him sick.

**3.** She experienced something that was unforgettable.

**4.** She heard something that was unbelievable.

**5.** They learned something that would always be useful.

**6.** They offered us something to eat that was unrecognizable.

**7.** They gave her something that would help her escape.

**8.** She said something that amused them.

**9.** He saw something which looked like a UFO.

**10.** They had to do things that seemed like a waste of time.

### Exercise 4

*What* is sometimes used for emphasis.

You need a vacation.
*What you need is a vacation.*

They ought to save more money.
*What they ought to do is save more money.*

Continue.

**1.** I love the way the food is presented. ...........................

**2.** I want a tall glass of water. ........................................

**3.** We have to work harder. ...........................................

**4.** They need a kick in the pants. ....................................

**5.** We should practice more. ..........................................

**6.** He needs more exercise. ...........................................

# Unit 63

**Language Summary**

whatever, whichever, whoever, whenever, wherever, however

*When should I do that? It doesn't matter. Do it whenever you like./Whenever you like.*

*What should I do? I don't care. Do whatever you want./Whatever you want.*

*Where should I put this? I don't know. Put it wherever you want./Wherever you want.*

*Who should I ask? It doesn't matter. Ask whoever is there./Whoever is there.*

*Which one should I take? I'm not sure. Take whichever one you like./Whichever one you like.*

*How should I do this? It isn't important. Do it however you like./However you like.*

## Exercise 1

Complete these ads using: whatever/whichever/whoever/whenever/wherever/however.

CLASSICAL, POP, JAZZ?

_____ you like your music,

it will sound better on a

**FONY STEREO.**

**LOCO COLA!**
YOU'LL FIND IT

_____

YOU GO.

**CENTRAL MOTORS' CALYPSO**

Choice of 7 models

_____ one you choose,

there's a five-year warranty.

_____ YOU'RE IN PORTSTOWN,
YOU **MUST** VISIT US.

THE
HONG KONG
**FOR THE BEST IN CHINESE FOOD**
501 Water St. Tel. 713-0121

TINKER, TAILOR, SOLDIER, SAILOR?
_____ you are,
there's something for you at the
**Municipal Art Museum.**

_____ *the weather,*
**Lushpuppy shoes** *take care*
*of your feet.*

## Exercise 2

Where can I put my coat? *It doesn't matter. Wherever you like.*

Continue.

**1.** When can I take my vacation? .........................................

**2.** Who should I invite to the party? .........................................

**3.** How should I cook the chicken? .........................................

**4.** What should I wear to the party? .........................................

**5.** Which color should I get? .........................................

**6.** Where can I park the car? .........................................

## Mr. Jones

During the winter of 1945 I lived for several months in a rooming house in Brooklyn. It was not a shabby place, but a pleasantly furnished, elderly brownstone kept hospital-neat by its owners, two maiden sisters.

Mr. Jones lived in the room next to mine. My room was the smallest in the house, his the largest, a nice big sunshiny room, which was just as well, for Mr. Jones never left it: all his needs, meals, shopping, laundry were attended to by the middle-aged landladies. Also, he was not without visitors; on the average, a half-dozen various persons, men and women, young, old, in-between, visited his room each day, from early morning until late in the evening. He was not a drug dealer or a fortune-teller; no, they came just to talk to him and apparently they made him small gifts of money for his conversation and advice. If not, he had no obvious means of support.

I never had a conversation with Mr. Jones myself, a circumstance I've often since regretted. He was a handsome man, about forty. Slender, black-haired, and with a distinctive face: a pale, lean face, high cheekbones, and with a birthmark on his left cheek, a small scarlet defect shaped like a star. He wore gold-rimmed glasses with pitch-black lenses: he was blind, and crippled, too—according to the sisters, the use of his legs had been denied him by a childhood accident, and he could not move without crutches. He was always dressed in a crisply pressed dark grey or blue three-piece suit and a subdued tie—as though about to set off for a Wall Street office.

However, as I've said, he never left the premises, simply sat in his cheerful room in a comfortable chair and received visitors. I had no notion of why they came to see him, these rather ordinary-looking folk, or what they talked about, and I was far too concerned with my own affairs to much wonder over it. When I did, I imagined that his friends had found in him an intelligent, kindly man, a good listener in whom to confide and consult with over their troubles: a cross between a priest and a therapist.

Mr. Jones had a telephone. He was the only tenant with a private line. It rang constantly, often after midnight and as early as six in the morning.

I moved to Manhattan. Several months later I returned to the house to collect a box of books I had stored there. While the landladies offered me tea and cakes in their lace-curtained "parlor," I inquired of Mr. Jones.

The women lowered their eyes. Clearing her throat, one said, "It's in the hands of the police."

The other offered, "We've reported him as a missing person."

The first added, "Last month, twenty-six days ago, my sister carried up Mr. Jones's breakfast, as usual. He wasn't there. All his belongings were there. But he was gone."

"It's odd—"

"—how a man totally blind, a helpless cripple—"

Ten years pass.

Now it is a zero-cold December afternoon, and I am in Moscow. I am riding in a subway car. There are only a few other passengers. One of them is a man sitting opposite me, a man wearing boots, a thick long coat and a Russian-style fur cap. He has bright eyes, blue as a peacock's.

After a doubtful instant, I simply stared, for even without the black glasses, there was no mistaking that lean distinctive face, those high cheekbones with the single star-shaped birthmark.

I was just about to cross the aisle and speak to him when the train pulled into a station, and Mr. Jones, on a pair of fine sturdy legs, stood up and strode out of the car. Swiftly, the train door closed behind him.

from *Music for Chameleons* by Truman Capote

### Exercise 1

Find words that mean:

1. a house where you can rent rooms
2. unable to see
3. unable to walk
4. someone who sells drugs
5. unmarried
6. bright red
7. sticks of wood or metal, used to help someone who has difficulty walking
8. unsure
9. curved pieces of glass used in glasses
10. a person who pays rent for a room or house
11. strong
12. a telephone
13. a person who treats illnesses, either physical or mental
14. softly, quietly colored
15. with little fat
16. the financial district of New York, particularly for the stock market
17. slim, thin
18. worn out, in bad condition
19. building
20. walked quickly

### Exercise 2

Glasses with gold rims are *gold-rimmed glasses*.
A person who tells your fortune is a *fortune-teller*.

Fill in the blanks below. All the words you will need are in the story.

1. A room with lace curtains is a ............ ............ room.
2. A suit with trousers, jacket, and a vest is a ............ ............ suit.
3. People who look ordinary are ............ ............ people.
4. A birthmark in the shape of a star is a ............ ............ birthmark.
5. A cap in a style which is worn in Russia is a ............ ............ cap.
6. A day which is very cold, with temperatures around 0°F, is a ............ ............ day.
7. A place which is as neat as a hospital is a ............ ............ place.
8. Lenses which are as black as pitch are ............ ............ lenses.
9. A woman in her forties or fifties is a ............ ............ woman.
10. A suit which has just been ironed and looks clean and fresh is a ............ ............ suit.
11. Instead of "six persons," you can say "a ............ ............ persons."
12. You can say that someone who is neither young nor old is ............ ............ .

### Exercise 3

1. "The use of his legs had been denied him by a childhood accident" means:
   □ **A.** He had been told that a childhood accident was not the cause of his injury.
   □ **B.** Because of a childhood accident, he couldn't walk.
   □ **C.** He had been forbidden to leave the house, after running over a child.

2. "He had no obvious means of support" means:
   □ **A.** Not many people seemed to like him.
   □ **B.** You couldn't see his crutches.
   □ **C.** Nobody knew how he got enough money to live on.

3. "I had no notion of why they came to see him" means:
   □ **A.** I never saw his visitors.
   □ **B.** I had no idea of the reason for their visits.
   □ **C.** He never told me why they came to see him.

4. "Clearing her throat" means:
   □ **A.** She coughed slightly.
   □ **B.** She touched her throat with her hand.
   □ **C.** She had a drink of water.

5. "It's in the hands of the police" means:
   □ **A.** The police are investigating it.
   □ **B.** The police came and took him away.
   □ **C.** He's in prison.

## TWO SUPERS:
# Johnny Dempsey
# Out With Claudia Powell

Hunky superstar Johnny Dempsey was seen out last night at the
House of Blues in Los Angeles with gorgeous supermodel Claudia
Powell. She had recently been engaged to singer David Dickens,
but the two broke up last week. Dickens could not be reached for comment.

**Exercise**

All of these are photos of celebrities taken by paparazzi. Write a headline and the first paragraph of a
newspaper story about each one.

*Susan Kohl (actress) and husband
Jonathan McCaffrey (director)*

...................................................................................................................................
...................................................................................................................................
...................................................................................................................................
...................................................................................................................................
...................................................................................................................................
...................................................................................................................................
...................................................................................................................................
...................................................................................................................................
...................................................................................................................................
...................................................................................................................................

*Margot Cherry (figure skater)*

...................................................................................................................................
...................................................................................................................................
...................................................................................................................................
...................................................................................................................................
...................................................................................................................................
...................................................................................................................................
...................................................................................................................................
...................................................................................................................................
...................................................................................................................................
...................................................................................................................................

*Nick West (actor)*

...................................................................................................................................
...................................................................................................................................
...................................................................................................................................
...................................................................................................................................
...................................................................................................................................
...................................................................................................................................
...................................................................................................................................
...................................................................................................................................
...................................................................................................................................

## THE MARTIANS ARE COMING

At eight o'clock on the evening of Sunday, October 30, 1938, thousands of Americans tuned in to CBS radio for "The Mercury Theater of the Air." Just after the program began it was interrupted by what sounded like the weather forecast. A minute or so later it was replaced by a program of dance music. Suddenly a solemn voice came over the air to warn Americans, "Ladies and gentlemen. I have a grave announcement to make...."

The speaker then went on to describe how strange beings from the planet Mars had landed in North America. They were using poisonous gas and death-ray machines to sweep all resistance before them in a series of bloody battles. The U.S.A. was being taken over by creatures from outer space!

The broadcast continued with a confusing series of announcements, often broken by long, chilling silences. The voice of the president was heard appealing to people not to panic. An announcer on top of a skyscraper in New York described how Manhattan was being overrun. His commentary broke off in a horrible, strangled scream.

That was the end of the program. Its producer, Orson Welles, and the cast of actors left the studio. They had completed their radio play, which had been based on War of the Worlds, a science-fiction novel by H.G. Wells. They didn't realize what effect their play had had. Thousands of people had fled from their homes. The roads were jammed with cars racing for the hills. Some of the cars were piled high with furniture. National Guardsmen rushed to volunteer to defend the world. Sailors in the U.S. Navy were recalled to their ships in New York harbor. Switchboards were completely jammed with people trying to call relatives and friends. In the South, people were praying in the streets. Some people even claimed that they had seen the Martians. The next morning's newspapers revealed that it had only been a radio play. It had all been a terrible mistake.

## Exercise 1

Find words or phrases which mean:

1. to adjust the controls of a radio or TV to a particular station
2. two words, both of which mean "serious"
3. containing a substance that can cause illness or death
4. opposition
5. machines designed to kill people by using radiation
6. a program sent out by radio or TV
7. a period without sound, which makes you feel cold with fear
8. to act out of fright without thinking clearly
9. a very tall building
10. a loud, high-pitched cry from pain or fear
11. the group of people acting in a play or movie
12. tightly filled
13. many things placed on top of each other
14. to protect from attack
15. a panel used for making connections by telephone
16. to make known

## Exercise 2

Complete this table.

| begin | began | begun |
|---|---|---|
| ................................... | left | ................................... |
| ................................... | ................................... | fled |
| ................................... | swept | ................................... |
| ................................... | overran | ................................... |
| see | ................................... | ................................... |
| ................................... | ................................... | come |
| take | ................................... | ................................... |
| ................................... | ................................... | heard |
| ................................... | was | ................................... |

## Exercise 3

Write full answers to these questions.

1. What was the name of the program?
2. Who was it produced by?
3. What novel was it based on?
4. Who was the novel written by?
5. What kind of novel was it?
6. Was the program really interrupted by the weather forecast?
7. Do you think it was really the president's voice?
8. Where was the announcer?
9. What might listeners have thought had happened to him?
10. What did the National Guardsmen do?
11. What happened to the switchboards?
12. Had any people actually seen the Martians?

# Unit 67

## Language Summary

*I'd rather go there.*

| *I'd rather* | *you* *he* *she* *we* *they* | *went there.* *didn't go there.* |

*It's time to go.*

| *It's (about) time* | *we* | *left.* *were leaving.* |

| *It isn't* | *as* | *if* *though* | *this were my first visit.* *he didn't know.* |

---

**Exercise 1**

**A:** How about going out for dinner tonight?

(B doesn't want to, so he says he'd rather do something else.)

| **B:** *I'd rather not. I'd rather* | *watch television.* *you made dinner here.* *we ordered a pizza.* |

Continue.

**1. A:** Let's go for a walk.

   **B:** ........................................................................

**2. A:** Why don't we go to the movies tonight?

   **B:** ........................................................................

**3. A:** We've won $20,000. We can buy a new car!

   **B:** ........................................................................

**4. A:** Do you want to go to Jamaica for our vacation?

   **B:** ........................................................................

**Exercise 2**

I'm not a child, you know.
*It isn't as if I were a child, you know.*

Continue.

**1.** I didn't do it deliberately.

........................................................................................

**2.** I'm not stupid, you know.

........................................................................................

**3.** I'm not a millionaire, you know.

........................................................................................

**4.** I don't come late every day!

........................................................................................

**Exercise 3**

Read all the sentences carefully. Read all the responses below.
Put the letter for the most appropriate response in the blanks provided.

**1:** Should we run? .......

**2:** I have 9:35 .......

**3:** Bye! .......

**4:** Can you take a message? .......

**5:** Do you want to stop for coffee?

   .......

**6:** Are you ready yet? .......

**7:** You're late. .......

**8:** Mark's just arrived. .......

**9:** You wash the dishes today. .......

**10:** Did you miss the beginning? .......

**11:** Is it time to go? .......

**12:** When will you have the money?

   .......

**13:** He's playing the trombone. .......

**14:** What time is dinner? .......

**15:** What's the delay? .......

**A:** Oh, not for another hour at least.
**B:** Yes, it's getting late.
**C:** No, we don't really have time.
**D:** I have 9:40.
**E:** Oh, no, not at this time of night!
**F:** Hold on. Let me get a pencil.
**G:** It's about time!

**H:** No, there's no need to hurry.
**I:** See you later.
**J:** I was just about to do them, dear.
**K:** Almost. I won't be long.
**L:** No, we were just in time.

**M:** Sorry, we couldn't find a parking space.
**N:** Well, it'll take me a long time to save that much.
**O:** It always takes forever and a day during rush hour.

## HELP THE POLICE HELP YOU

Your police force needs your help in beating crime. They can't do their job without it. You can help best by immediately reporting anything that seems suspicious.

If you saw someone being attacked or robbing a store you would naturally phone the police. But call them just the same if you see someone lurking around your neighbor's back door or trying car doors. The police won't mind if you are wrong. And call right away—seconds count!

What you should do:

Dial 911, Emergency Services. Tell them as much as you can:

1. Where the incident occurred.
2. The number of people involved.
3. Descriptions of the suspects.
4. Description of the scene.
5. License numbers of any vehicles involved.
6. Your name and address will help, but they are not essential.

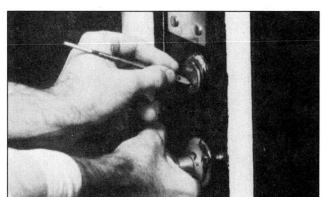

### Exercise 1

Read the text at the left and the "anti-theft" questionnaire below. Ask another student the questions, and answer the questionnaire.

### Exercise 2

Read the text again. Imagine you are walking past a neighbor's house. You know your neighbor is on vacation. A window is open. You see a man and a woman get into a truck outside the house and drive away. Now call the police. Look at the instructions, and report the incident to them.

.......................................................................................................
.......................................................................................................
.......................................................................................................
.......................................................................................................
.......................................................................................................
.......................................................................................................
.......................................................................................................
.......................................................................................................
.......................................................................................................

## Anti-Theft Check

You should be able to answer "yes" to all these questions. If you can't, take immediate steps so that you will be able to do so. And remember, when in doubt, ask at your police station for your Crime Prevention Officer. It's free advice.

| General precautions | yes | no |
| --- | --- | --- |
| 1. Do you stop your newspaper subscription when you're going to be away? | ❑ | ❑ |
| 2. Do you always lock your garage door when you take the car out? | ❑ | ❑ |
| 3. When you're out for the evening, do you lock all the outside doors and leave a light on in a front room? | ❑ | ❑ |
| 4. When you go out, do you lock all the windows? | ❑ | ❑ |
| 5. If you go on vacation, do you ask a neighbor to keep an eye on the house? | ❑ | ❑ |
| 6. Do you tell the police when you're going to be away and who has the spare key? | ❑ | ❑ |
| 7. Do you lock your tool shed when you're not using it? | ❑ | ❑ |

| Locks | yes | no |
| --- | --- | --- |
| 8. Are all outside doors fitted with good quality dead-bolt locks? | ❑ | ❑ |
| 9. Are all your windows fitted with suitable locks or alarms? | ❑ | ❑ |

| Your property | yes | no |
| --- | --- | --- |
| 10. Have you photographed all your valuable possessions or jewelry? | ❑ | ❑ |
| 11. Do you have a list of the serial numbers of your TV set, radio, camera, etc.? | ❑ | ❑ |
| 12. Do you always lock your bicycle when you leave it? | ❑ | ❑ |

| Your car | yes | no |
| --- | --- | --- |
| 13. Is your car equipped with an alarm? | ❑ | ❑ |
| 14. Do you always take the keys with you when you leave the car? | ❑ | ❑ |
| 15. Do you lock the trunk and the doors and roll up the windows when you leave the car? | ❑ | ❑ |
| 16. Do you remove all valuables before you leave the car? | ❑ | ❑ |

# Unit 69

## Language Summary

| It/They | is/are<br>was/were<br>has/have been<br>is/are being<br>will be<br>can be<br>may be<br>has/have to be | done. |
|---|---|---|

## Exercise 1

Fill in the blanks in this text. Use the correct forms of these verbs. Use each verb only once.

| auction off | claim | discover | find | go through |
|---|---|---|---|---|
| hand in | keep | leave | turn in | wrap |

Thousands of objects are left in New York City Transit Authority vehicles every year. Some of them are .................. and are .................. at the Transit Authority Lost and Found Office. Some of the lost items are .................. ; those that are not are .................. . Umbrellas, hats, and toys are the most common items, but some very strange things have been .................. . A stuffed life-size gorilla was .................. sitting on a subway seat. A wheelchair was left in a bus. Human bones, which were .................. in brown paper, were .................. to an astonished bus driver. Glasses and false teeth are sometimes .................. by the people who find them, and this can create a problem when the owner comes to pick them up. One man arrived to claim an upper set of false teeth. Hundreds of sets were .................. before he found the set that matched his lower set.

## Exercise 2

The president gave a speech on television last night. These are some of the things
that were said. Change them to the passive.

You elected me two years ago.
*I was elected two years ago.*

**1.** I chose qualified people for the Cabinet. .........................
.................................................................................

**2.** We have achieved many things since then. ..................
.................................................................................

**3.** We reduced personal income taxes a year ago. ............
.................................................................................

**4.** We are beating inflation. ..............................................
.................................................................................

**5.** However, we can't do everything at the same time. ......
.................................................................................

**6.** We have to make some hard choices. ..........................
.................................................................................

**7.** We hold regular meetings with leaders of management
and labor unions ............................................................
.................................................................................

**8.** We may achieve a 3% growth rate next year. ..............
.................................................................................

## Exercise 3

After the employees of Orion Publishing Co. leave work for the day, the cleaning crew comes in. They have to clean the rest rooms, wash out the coffeemakers, put away any milk or sugar that has been left out, empty the wastebaskets, vacuum the carpets, and wash the floors. When the employees return each morning, this is what they find: *The rest rooms have been cleaned.*

Write five more sentences.

**1.** ....................................................................

**2.** ....................................................................

**3.** ....................................................................

**4.** ....................................................................

**5.** ....................................................................

## Language Summary

*It was being done.*     *It had been done.*

### Westwood Productions
— Hollywood CA —

**Movie:** Bandido          **Producer:** Samuel Goldheim
**Director:** Charles Orson   **Chief Camera Operator:** Paul Entacks
**Date:** Tuesday, July 7    **Scene:** #37 (Interior Silver Dollar Saloon)
**Filming begins at:** 8:45 a.m.

#### Pre-filming Schedule

| Time | Notes |
|---|---|
| 5:30 Assemble set | ✓ finished 7:00 |
| 5:45 Set up lighting | ✗ not yet completed |
| 6:15 Make up Rita Colon | ✓ completed by 7:15 |
|     Make up William Paine | ✓ done by 6:30 |
| 6:45 Put beard on Marvin Lee | ✗ not yet finished |
| 7:00 Dress, make up extras | IN PROGRESS |
| 7:20 Fix Ms. Colon's hair | IN PROGRESS |
| 7:20 Check furniture | IN PROGRESS |
| 8:15 Put bottles and glasses on tables | ✗ |
| 8:20 Set up microphones | ✗ |
| 8:30 Check camera positions | ✗ |

### Exercise 1

It's 7:30. Charles Orson has just arrived on the set of *Bandido,* his new Western. The assistant director has just shown him the checklist above and is explaining it to him.

*Orson: Has Ms. Colon's hair been fixed yet?*
*Assistant: I'm afraid not. It's being done right now.*

Write ten more exchanges like this.

### Exercise 2

Later that day, Charles Orson went to the producer to complain about the morning's arrangements.

*"When I got there, Rita's hair was still being fixed. The camera positions hadn't been checked."*

Write six more sentences.

**1.** ...........................................................................................................................................................................

.............................................................................................................................................................................

**2.** ...........................................................................................................................................................................

.............................................................................................................................................................................

**3.** ...........................................................................................................................................................................

.............................................................................................................................................................................

**4.** ...........................................................................................................................................................................

.............................................................................................................................................................................

**5.** ...........................................................................................................................................................................

.............................................................................................................................................................................

**6.** ...........................................................................................................................................................................

.............................................................................................................................................................................

The producer said, *"Well, what had been done?"*

Write three sentences.

**8.** ...........................................................................

**7.** ...............................................................     **9.** ...........................................................................

# Unit 71

## Language Summary

*There's a lot to be (done).*
*It will have to be (done)* | *by September.*
*It will have been (done)* | *in two years' time.*
| *before the end of the year.*

The Republic of Wibalandia is building a new capital, Banyaville. It's being built on the banks of the Banya River. It was started five years ago, and three projects have already been finished. The government hopes that it will be finished in about ten years' time. They hope to move to Banyaville in about five years' time, although many buildings won't have been completed by then. There will still be a lot to be done.

| BANYAVILLE CONSTRUCTION SCHEDULE | | |
| --- | --- | --- |
| **Project** | **Status/ Expected Start Date** | **Expected Completion** |
| Highway 1 | completed three yrs. ago | |
| Banya Bridge | completed three yrs. ago | |
| Highway 2 | construction under way | rainy season this yr. |
| National Library | next yr. | 4 yrs. |
| University | construction under way | 5 yrs. |
| National Hospital | next mo. | 4 yrs. |
| Airport | one | |
| open | 3 yrs. | |
| Bus Terminal | construction began last yr. | Sept. |
| Parliament Building | foundations laid last yr. | 2 yrs. |
| Ministry of Education | construction under way | 4 yrs. |
| Ministry of the Interior | construction under way | 7 mos. |
| Ministry of Foreign Affairs | next wk. | 18 mos. |
| President's Palace | next yr. | 3 yrs. |
| Kawee Bridge | construction under way | next Jan. |

## Exercise 1

Answer these questions in full.

1. Where is the capital being built?

2. When was it started?

3. How many projects have been finished?

4. When will it all be finished?

5. When will the government move there?

6. Will everything have been completed?

7. How much will there be left to be done?

## Exercise 2

The National Library *will have to be started next year if it is to be completed on time.*

Write similar sentences about:

1. The National Hospital ......................................................
......................................................................................

2. The Ministry of Foreign Affairs .........................................
......................................................................................

3. The President's Palace ...................................................
......................................................................................

## Exercise 3

A spokesperson for the government was interviewed on the news recently. She said, "There's still a lot to be done. There's a highway to be finished. There's a library to be built."

Write seven more sentences using *There's (something) to be finished* and three more sentences using *There's (something) to be built.*

## Exercise 4

*The Ministry of Education will have been completed/built/finished in four years' time.*

Write sentences using *will have been (done)* about:

1. Highway 2
2. The airport
3. The National Hospital
4. The bus terminal
5. The Ministry of Foreign Affairs
6. The Kawee Bridge
7. The Winkee Bridge
8. The National Library
9. The Ministry of the Interior
10. The President's Palace

# Unit 72

**Language Summary**

*to have/get something done*
*It needs doing.*
*It needs to be done.*

## Exercise 1

Look at the words in the box. Read them all carefully. Write eight sentences like this.

*(His) hair needed cutting, so (he) went to the hair stylist's to get it cut.*

| | | |
|---|---|---|
| watch | Department of | tune up |
| driver's license | Motor Vehicles | renew |
| hair | garage | wash |
| suit | camera store | change |
| shoes | clinic | repair |
| shirts | laundry | press |
| film | jewelry store | shine |
| bandage | dry cleaners | cut |
| car | hair stylist's | develop |
| | shoe repair shop | |

1. ...................................................................................
...................................................................................
2. ...................................................................................
...................................................................................
3. ...................................................................................
4. ...................................................................................
5. ...................................................................................
6. ...................................................................................
7. ...................................................................................
8. ...................................................................................

## Exercise 2

Look at the words in the box. Write eight sentences like this.

*(She's) going to an architect to have (her) house designed.*

| | | |
|---|---|---|
| pharmacist | palm | alter |
| photographer's | suit | X-ray |
| studio | house | photocopy |
| eye doctor | portrait | fill |
| fortune teller | chest | test |
| architect | prescription | design |
| copy center | eyes | read |
| artist | documents | paint |
| tailor | picture | take |
| clinic | | |

1. ...................................................................................
...................................................................................
2. ...................................................................................
...................................................................................
3. ...................................................................................
4. ...................................................................................
5. ...................................................................................
6. ...................................................................................
7. ...................................................................................
8. ...................................................................................

BERMUDA

## GENERAL INFORMATION
There are about 150 small islands which comprise Bermuda. The seven largest of them are connected by bridges and causeways, and, in the absence of "outer" islands, it is this contiguous conformation of land which has given rise to the singular appellation "Island of Bermuda."

## CURRENCY
Legal tender in Bermuda is the Bermuda Dollar (BD$), which is divided into 100 cents. The Bermuda dollar is pegged to the US dollar on an equal (1 to 1) basis.

This means that US currency is accepted at shops, restaurants, and hotels at equal (face) value. Other foreign currencies are not accepted but may be exchanged at local banks at rates that are set daily.

US traveller's cheques are accepted everywhere.

Foreign personal cheques may be cashed at some hotels and shops. The cashing of foreign personal cheques at the banks may be negotiated by special arrangement. Business establishments will not normally cash them.

## LANGUAGE
Bermuda is an English-speaking country. The only other language spoken by a small section of the community is Portuguese. A number of the larger hotel establishments employ staff members from Western Europe and other countries who speak a variety of languages other than English.

### PUBLIC HOLIDAYS

| | |
|---|---|
| New Year's Day | January 1 |
| Good Friday | date varies (in March or April) |
| Bermuda Day | May 24 |
| Queen's Birthday | the third Monday in June |
| Cup Match | the first Thursday in August |
| Somers Day | the first Friday in August |
| Labour Day | the first Monday in September |
| Remembrance Day | November 11 |
| Christmas Day | December 25 |
| Boxing Day | December 26 |

## CLIMATE
Bermuda is located 890 miles (1,432 km) off the coast of South Carolina, with the Gulf Stream flowing in between Bermuda and the United States. It is not a tropical island, but a semi-tropical one. Bermuda has two seasons—spring and summer.

**Summer** temperatures are usually from late May to mid-November, with the warmest weather in July, August, and the first half of September. During the warmest months the thermometer generally does not rise above 89°F (32°C), and the evening temperatures are generally about 10°F (5°C) lower.

**Spring** temperatures, from mid-November through April, vary from the seventies Fahrenheit (low twenties Centigrade) to the sixties Fahrenheit (mid-teens Centigrade). January, February, and early March are the coolest months, but even then there are often comfortable sunny days. There is excellent swimming in Bermuda when the temperature is in the seventies Fahrenheit (low twenties Centigrade) and the average sea temperature does not go below the sixties Fahrenheit (mid-teens Centigrade).

**Change of Season:** mid-November to mid-December, and late March through April, either spring or summer weather may occur.

**Rainfall:** there is no rainy season in Bermuda as such; rainfall is spread fairly evenly throughout the year. For the most part, rain occurs in squalls which pass quite quickly; all-day rains are not frequent, but there may be several days in a row when squalls—interspersed with sunny conditions—pass over the island. Traditionally, the summers are dryer than the winters, but weather conditions can never be guaranteed.

**Hurricanes:** As hurricanes move north toward the U.S. from the Caribbean area to the south, Bermuda occasionally feels their effects in the form of high winds and rougher seas. In the past 10 years, very few hurricanes passing northward have brought winds of hurricane force, so they should not be a cause of concern to prospective visitors.

Weather Observations Over a ten-year period (1984–1993)
Monthly average daily temperatures and rainfall. Temperatures in Centigrade & Fahrenheit

| | Jan. | Feb. | Mar. | Apr. | May | June | July | Aug. | Sep. | Oct. | Nov. | Dec. |
|---|---|---|---|---|---|---|---|---|---|---|---|---|
| Air Temp. °C Maximum | 20.7 | 20.4 | 20.8 | 21.9 | 24.8 | 26.9 | 29.2 | 29.8 | 29.0 | 26.6 | 24.2 | 21.6 |
| °F | 69.2 | 68.7 | 69.4 | 71.4 | 76.7 | 80.4 | 84.5 | 85.6 | 84.2 | 79.8 | 75.5 | 70.9 |
| Air Temp. °C Minimum | 15.7 | 15.1 | 15.5 | 16.6 | 18.7 | 21.9 | 23.8 | 24.3 | 23.3 | 21.6 | 19.3 | 16.3 |
| °F | 60.3 | 59.1 | 59.9 | 61.9 | 65.6 | 71.5 | 74.9 | 75.7 | 73.9 | 70.8 | 66.8 | 61.3 |
| Sea Temp. °C Average | 18.0 | 17.8 | 18.5 | 20.7 | 24.0 | 26.3 | 28.3 | 28.9 | 26.5 | 24.2 | 21.2 | 19.3 |
| °F | 64.4 | 64.4 | 65.3 | 69.3 | 75.2 | 79.3 | 82.9 | 84.0 | 79.7 | 75.6 | 70.2 | 66.7 |
| Relative Humidity % | 77.6 | 76.2 | 75.3 | 78.3 | 81.7 | 84.9 | 83.9 | 80.7 | 79.5 | 81.2 | 78.5 | 78.0 |
| Rainfall cm | 15.2 | 11.9 | 11.7 | 11.4 | 5.8 | 10.4 | 10.2 | 10.4 | 12.2 | 14.2 | 9.4 | 11.4 |
| inches | 6.0 | 4.7 | 4.6 | 4.5 | 2.3 | 4.1 | 4.0 | 4.1 | 4.8 | 5.6 | 3.7 | 4.5 |

Courtesy of the Bermuda Department of Tourism

## Exercise 1

Read the text and answer these questions. (Note: British spellings have been used in the text.)

**1.** How far is Bermuda from New York?

**2.** How far is it from London?

**3.** How many islands are there?

**4.** How many Bermuda dollars are equal to five U.S. dollars?

**5.** Where in Bermuda are U.S. traveler's checks accepted?

**6.** Is any language other than English spoken there?

**7.** Does your country have more or fewer national holidays?

**8.** Is Bermuda's climate tropical?

**9.** Which are the hottest months?

**10.** Which are the coldest months?

**11.** Which is the wettest month?

**12.** Which is the drier season?

**13.** Which are the best months for swimming?

**14.** Should you pack an umbrella with you? Why or why not?

**15.** What sometimes happens in Bermuda when hurricanes move from the Caribbean north toward the United States?

## Exercise 2

Read the text and describe your country/state in a similar way. Include information about the geography, currency, language, and climate. (Write about 300 words.)

# Unit 74

## Language Summary

| Tell, ask, remind, invite, advise, help, warn, instruct, order, urge, force, beg | (someone) | to do (something). not to do (something). |
|---|---|---|

---

### Exercise 1

"If I were you, I'd go to the dentist."

*He/She advised me/him/her to go to the dentist.*

Look at the Language Summary. Use each of the 12 reporting verbs once only.

**1.** "If I were you, I wouldn't carry so much money."

..................................................................

**2.** "Meet me at the French Roast Cafe at 8:15."

..................................................................

**3.** "Put on the right turn signal, get into the right lane, and turn right."

..................................................................

**4.** "Would you wait outside for a few minutes, please?"

..................................................................

**5.** "Don't forget to turn off the lights and lock the door."

..................................................................

**6.** "You should definitely try out for the part."

..................................................................

**7.** "You'd better not park here. It's dangerous."

..................................................................

**8.** "Let me put that suitcase on the rack for you."

..................................................................

**9.** "Would you like to come with us to get a cup of coffee?"

..................................................................

**10.** "Oh please, don't leave me! I need you!"

..................................................................

**11.** "Show me your driver's license. I'm a police officer."

..................................................................

**12.** "This is a gun. Give me the money, slowly. That's right."

..................................................................

---

### Exercise 2

He reminded her to go to the post office.

*"Don't forget to go to the post office."*

**1.** She reminded him to set the alarm.

..................................................................

**2.** He told us to get off at the next station and transfer to the Blue Line.

..................................................................

**3.** They begged her to help them.

..................................................................

**4.** He invited them to visit the school.

..................................................................

**5.** She instructed him to turn off the CD player.

..................................................................

**6.** He urged her to go to the hospital.

..................................................................

**7.** She warned them not to eat it because it was poisonous.

..................................................................

**8.** She ordered them to get out of the car with their hands up.

..................................................................

**9.** They asked us to explain it again.

..................................................................

**10.** They forced him to open the safe.

..................................................................

## Language Summary

Reporting statements

**Exercise 1**

*Mr. and Mrs. N. said that they had enjoyed themselves enormously.*

Continue.

1. ...................................................................................................................................................
2. ...................................................................................................................................................
3. ...................................................................................................................................................
4. ...................................................................................................................................................
5. ...................................................................................................................................................
6. ...................................................................................................................................................
7. ...................................................................................................................................................
8. ...................................................................................................................................................
9. ...................................................................................................................................................

**Exercise 2**

### CONTINTENTAL COMPUTERS, INC
#### 1994 ANNUAL REPORT OF THE BOARD OF DIRECTORS

We are pleased to announce that 1994 has been a very good year for the company. Overall sales have increased 20% and most of the increase has been in exports. There is great demand for our TX range of computers, and we will be developing a larger version next year. Our two main plants are working at full capacity and our Palo Alto plant is being enlarged.

We are fairly optimistic about the future although much will depend on the value of the dollar and world trading conditions. We have repaid most of the money borrowed from the banks last year. However, we are still able to announce increased profits and an increased dividend of 51¢ per share. We are also offering one free share for every four held.

Report the Board of Directors' statement, beginning:

*The Board said that they were pleased ....*

# Unit 76

## Language Summary

Reporting questions

*He asked me what time it was. I said it was six.*
*She asked me if I had enjoyed myself. I said I had.*

### Exercise

When Deborah Medina arrived at Kennedy Airport in New York, she was stopped by a market researcher who asked her some questions. Look at the completed form, and report the questions and answers.

**1.** What's your name?

   **A.** *He asked her what her name was.*

   **B.** *She said it was Deborah Medina.*

**2.** Are you American?

   **A.** ........................................................................

   **B.** ........................................................................

**3.** How old are you?

   **A.** ........................................................................

   **B.** ........................................................................

**4.** Which airport did you fly from?

   **A.** ........................................................................

   **B.** ........................................................................

**5.** Did you fly People Air?

   **A.** ........................................................................

   **B.** ........................................................................

**6.** Can you tell me the flight number?

   **A.** ........................................................................

   **B.** ........................................................................

**7.** Did you travel first class?

   **A.** ........................................................................

   **B.** ........................................................................

**8.** Have you been away on vacation or business?

   **A.** ........................................................................

   **B.** ........................................................................

**9.** How long will you be in New York?

   **A.** ........................................................................

   **B.** ........................................................................

**10.** Will you be staying in a hotel?

   **A.** ........................................................................

   **B.** ........................................................................

**11.** How are you getting home?

   **A.** ........................................................................

   **B.** ........................................................................

---

## MARKET RESEARCH
## KENNEDY AIRPORT PASSENGER SURVEY

1. NAME: Deborah Medina

2. NATIONALITY: U.S.

3. AGE: 38

4. AIRPORT OF DEPARTURE: Narita Airport, Tokyo

5. AIRLINE: People Air        6. Flight No.: 900

7. FARE BASIS:        __ 1st class    ✓ Business Class    __ Coach
                      __ Charter      __ Standby

8. PURPOSE OF TRAVEL: __ Vacation    ✓ Business __ Educational
                      __ Family reasons __ Relocation __ Other

9. LENGTH OF STAY: ✓ Returning home      __ Overnight
                   __ Less than one week __ Less than one month
                   __ More than one month

10. WHERE WILL YOU BE STAYING: ✓ Home __ Hotel    __ Motel
                               __ With friends or relatives
                               __ Other

    If hotel or motel, please specify where:
    _____

11. MEANS OF TRANSPORTATION: __Bus    __Subway    __ Rental car
                             __ Taxi/Limousine    ✓ Private car

## Language Summary

Reporting conversations
The use of reporting verbs other than *say, ask,* and *tell.*

---

### Exercise 1

She invited him to a party.

*Would you like to come to a party next weekend?*
or *We're having a party tomorrow. Can you come?*
or *I hope you'll able to come to my party on Friday.*

Write sentences like these for the following:

**1.** She agreed to sign the contract.

**2.** He greeted them formally.

**3.** She arranged to meet them at midnight.

**4.** She complimented him on his cooking.

**5.** The driver wanted the tank filled and the oil checked.

**6.** She thanked them warmly for their presents.

**7.** He admitted that he hadn't been telling the truth.

**8.** The actress refused to answer any more questions.

**9.** She offered to drive him home.

**10.** He explained that he had lost his way.

---

### Exercise 2

Report these sentences. Use each of the verbs in the box below once.

| | | |
|---|---|---|
| remember | deny | add |
| apologize | invite | exclaim |
| suggest | beg | admit |
| hear | | |

**1.** Would you like to go for a walk?

**2.** We could go to that new Italian restaurant.

**3.** Oh, my God! It's you!

**4.** Oh yes, the little hotel overlooking the bay.

**5.** And another thing. I think you're selfish.

**6.** Please, please, don't turn the light off.

**7.** I'm terribly sorry I'm late.

**8.** I really didn't do anything wrong.

**9.** There will be a new prize next month. It was on TV.

**10.** All right. It was me. I did it.

---

### Exercise 3

This is an extract from page 122 of *Trust the Heart.* Fill in the blanks using each of these verbs once.

| | | |
|---|---|---|
| asked | promised | whispered |
| shouted | said | replied |
| cried | exclaimed | murmured |
| interrupted | | |

Don stood at the gate, in the crowded passenger waiting area, gazing through the dirty window at the planes parked outside. Where was Melissa? She had ........................ to come to say good-bye. The plane was due to board in a few moments. Then he saw her, the morning sunlight dancing in her hair.
"Don!" she ........................, "Don!"
"Melissa...!" he ........................ softly, "I thought that—"
She ........................ him. "You thought I wouldn't come. I know that."
"Oh, no. I was just afraid that..." His voice shook with emotion. "I had to come," she ........................ "In spite of everything, I had to."
"I'm so glad. But is this good-bye forever?" he ........................ .
"You know what my conditions are," she ........................ .
"Yes, and I agreed to them, but you don't believe me. So, it is good-bye, then," he ........................ firmly.
"No, Don ... no," she ........................ . "I've decided to believe you—for now—so I've brought my suitcase, and I've bought a ticket on this flight. I'm going with you—if you still want me to."
"Melissa! My darling!" he ........................ . "Why, this is the most wonderful ... ."

# The Secrets of Living *Happily Ever After*

In her new book, *Happily Ever After,* author Laura Martin reveals the secrets of a happy marriage. Its message is up-beat and optimistic. We interviewed Martin at her home in Colorado.

**Q: How has marriage changed in the past fifty years?**

Life used to be much simpler, with fewer choices. When we look at marriages in the 1950s, most were of the "Father Knows Best" and "The Donna Reed Show" kind. The man was the breadwinner; the woman, the homemaker. There was also an optimism then—an expectation that you would do better economically than your own parents. Now, women often work outside the home, too. There are economic pressures to do so—it's not just a question of women wanting careers—and there are no guarantees of financial well-being. There's also a lot more stress to deal with outside of the family—international terrorism, drugs, diseases that were unheard of just a few decades ago. Often now, both partners spend their days in high-stress jobs in a more stressful world in general and come home to a lot of responsibilities—children, house, bills—to name a few. There's not a lot of time for each other, let alone for oneself.

**Q: You paint a pretty grim picture of life nowadays. Yet your book is optimistic. How come?**

I have faith in our ability to rise above the challenges of our times. I think there are some fundamental requirements, though, for a happy marriage. You can't live happily ever after unless you marry the right person in the first place.

**Q: What do you mean by "fundamental requirements"?**

You have to be in love with the person you marry. Of course, I don't mean you have to stay in that stage of being in love where all you can do is think about the other person! No. That stage in courtship lasts only a short time. But after the initial excitement subsides, you should still be in love. You also must totally respect the other person, and you should like him or her. You should also not need the other person to fulfill every one of your needs. Other people—friends, children, coworkers—have a place in your life, too. If you expect your partner to be everything for you, you're bound to be disappointed.

**Q: So, assuming you've met the fundamental requirements, what are the secrets to living happily ever after?**

Make time for each other. No matter how high-pressured your job, no matter how much time you need to devote to your children, set aside some time every day to be alone with each other. Ask each other how your day was and what's on your mind. Listen totally. When your partner has a problem, don't jump to solve it or dismiss it as unimportant. Let the other person talk it out and he or she may solve it alone or realize it's not important. Be your partner's best friend. And make sure to have intimate time alone together a few times a week. That's really important.

**Q: Anything else?**

Yes! I know this is going to sound like a contradiction, but give each other space, too. In other words, we need to be alone sometimes; some people need solitude more than others. Find out if your partner does, and find a way to accommodate this need. And speaking of needs, we all need to know we are loved, but we don't all need to have it expressed the same way. Some of us are auditory, some visual, some kinesthetic. The auditory people need to hear the words "I love you"; the visual people need to "see" it—like getting flowers or being taken out for dinner; the kinesthetic people need to be touched. Make sure you express your love in the way your partner needs you to.

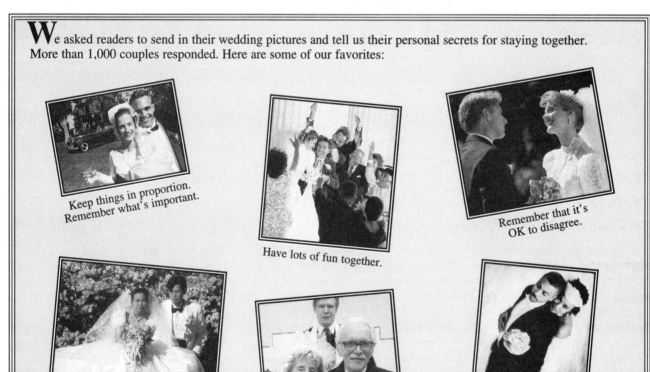

W e asked readers to send in their wedding pictures and tell us their personal secrets for staying together. More than 1,000 couples responded. Here are some of our favorites:

Keep things in proportion. Remember what's important.

Have lots of fun together.

Remember that it's OK to disagree.

Work on yourself alone so you're always becoming a better person.

Never go to bed mad at each other.

Go out on a date with each other once a week— no matter what!

## Exercise 1

Find words that mean:

1. the opposite of what you've just said
2. basic
3. time alone
4. meet the needs
5. tell
6. give

7. first
8. become less
9. likely
10. close, private
11. gloomy, unhappy
12. a person you work with

## Exercise 2

1. "Father Knows Best" and "The Donna Reed Show" are

   A. old TV shows

   B. old movies

   C. old books

2. "The man was the breadwinner; the woman, the homemaker" means:

   A. The man worked in a bakery, and the woman worked at home.

   B. The man did the grocery shopping, and the woman did the cooking.

   C. The man went out to work, and the woman stayed home to care for the house and children.

3. "It's not just a question of women wanting careers" means:

   A. Many men question the idea of women working.

   B. Many women want to continue their careers after they are married and have children.

   C. Women may want careers, but they give them up when they get married.

4. "What's on your mind" means:

   A. the things you're thinking about

   B. the things that annoy you

   C. the things you're dreaming about

5. "Give each other space" means:

   A. Don't stand too close to your partner.

   B. Go out at night together to look at the stars.

   C. Leave the other person alone sometimes.

## Exercise 3

What do you think are the secrets of a good marriage? (Write about 250 words.)

# British and American English

It has been said "England and America are two countries divided by a common language." However, the differences between British and American English are comparatively small. Although British newspapers occasionally publish letters from irate citizens complaining that they are unable to understand a word of the latest American TV series, it is clear that few people have serious problems. In fact, people on both sides of the Atlantic might have much more difficulty in understanding the stronger regional dialects of their own country than in understanding an average speaker from the other country. Television, movies, and poplular music have helped to bridge the Atlantic, and those minor difficulties which might occur in comprehension are probably much fewer than 40 or 50 years ago.

It is true that an American would say:

"Excuse me, do you have ... ?"

while in Britain it would be more common to say:

"Pardon me, have you got ... ?"

However, both forms would be understood in both countries.

One of the most obvious areas of difference would relate to words connected with driving, for example:

| American | British |
|---|---|
| car, auto | motor car |
| sedan | saloon |
| fender | wing |
| hood | bonnet |
| trunk | boot |
| station wagon | estate car |
| gas (gasoline) | petrol |
| gear shift | gear changer |
| driver's license | driving licence |

Of course, an American who asked for "gas" in England would get what he wanted, and someone from England could be fairly certain of getting "petrol." But other, less important or less commonly used words might present more of a problem.

## Exercise 1

Read the text above and write "A" for "American" or "B" for "British."

**1.** boot .......

**2.** gas ......

**3.** gear shift .......

**4.** filling station .......

**5.** petrol .......

**6.** accelerator .......

**7.** sedan .......

**8.** station wagon .......

**9.** gas station .......

**10.** hood .......

**11.** mailman .......

**12.** postman .......

## Exercise 2

Here are some pairs of words. One of each pair is more common in American English, the other in British English. Try to find out which one is American, and which is British. Put them in the correct columns:

potato chips/crisps
vacation/holiday
rare/underdone
drugstore/chemist's
lift/elevator
pavement/sidewalk
apartment/flat
motorway/highway

braces/suspenders
interval/intermission
conductor/guard
plimsolls/sneakers
pram/baby carriage
center/centre
theatre/theater
trailer/caravan

| American | British |
|---|---|
| ............................... | ............................... |
| ............................... | ............................... |
| ............................... | ............................... |
| ............................... | ............................... |
| ............................... | ............................... |
| ............................... | ............................... |
| ............................... | ............................... |
| ............................... | ............................... |
| ............................... | ............................... |
| ............................... | ............................... |
| ............................... | ............................... |
| ............................... | ............................... |
| ............................... | ............................... |
| ............................... | ............................... |
| ............................... | ............................... |
| ............................... | ............................... |

## Exercise 3

Look at the following examples of British English and rewrite them in American English.

**1.** Have you had your holiday yet? ......................................
................................................................................

**2.** Have you got a driving licence? ......................................
................................................................................

**3.** It's half past six. ...............................................................
................................................................................

**4.** Should I open the tin? ......................................................
................................................................................

**5.** He always helps me with the washing-up. ........................
................................................................................

**6.** He got in the train. ...........................................................
................................................................................

# Unit 80

**Exercise 1**

Read Unit 80 in the Student Book. Write a postcard from Yoshiko to Mr. Michael Berman, American English Institute, Sonoma State College, Sonoma, CA 95476 USA. As Yoshiko, thank him and all the other teachers for all the help they gave you. Say that with your improved English you will be able to get a good job. Promise to call and see them when you are in the States next year.

**Exercise 2**

Write a postcard from Yoshiko to Carlos Poveda Navas, Calle la Escuela, Quinta Chuao, Caracas 106, Venezuela. As Yoshiko, tell him where you are and tell him that you got a job. Ask about the other students in the class. Ask him if he passed his exam and invite him to visit you if he's ever in Tokyo. Remind him that he has your address and phone number.

**Exercise 3**

Write a letter from Yoshiko to her landlady, Mrs. Simmons. As Yoshiko, tell Mrs. Simmons that you had a pleasant flight and arrived safely. Apologize for not phoning. Thank her for everything she did and inquire about Mr. Simmons and "Milhous," the dog. Send your regards to one or two other people. Promise to visit them next summer when you will be in the States on vacation. Invite them to come and visit you in Tokyo. Assure them that they would be welcome. Promise to show them all the sights and say that you'll cook them a real Japanese dinner. Say that you very much hope they'll be able to come.

# Review

Read through Units 41–80 in the Student Book, and answer these questions.

**Unit**

**41.** Complete this saying: "An apple a day ..." ...............................................................................

**42.** What does Shirley wish she hadn't done? ..............................................................................

**43.** What is Anne Marie's only regret? ........................................................................................

**44.** What does Robin do? ............................................................................................................

**45.** What happened to 004? .........................................................................................................

**46.** Where did 006 go after Washington, and what did he do there? ............................................

**47.** What is a widower? ...............................................................................................................

**48.** What drug was banned by the FDA? .....................................................................................

**49.** Why is Greg Larkin writing to Les Gardner? .........................................................................

**50.** In what city does Aunt Molly live? .........................................................................................

**51.** Describe the room you are in right now. ................................................................................

**52.** Briefly describe your mother, father, sister, or brother. ........................................................

**53.** What does Ron Parrow know how to do? ...............................................................................

**54.** Why are the Ciprianis going to start their own construction business? ..................................

**55.** Why should you keep plastic bags away from babies? ...........................................................

**56.** Why was it easy for Luke to start conversations? .................................................................

**57.** How many people survived the *Hindenburg* disaster? ...........................................................

**58.** Why did Eric Miller have a milk shake? .................................................................................

**59.** Give directions from Huntington to the Smithsonian on the Metro. ........................................

**60.** Why was the Portstown High School stadium filled last night? ..............................................

**61.** Which are increasing, the number of marriages or the number of suicides? .........................

**62.** Why doesn't Bo want to talk about business? .......................................................................

**63.** Where can Alan park his motorcycle? ...................................................................................

**64.** Where would you go if you wanted to change the shape of your nose? .................................

**65.** What are photographers called who specialize in taking pictures of celebrities? ..................

**66.** What did *Voyager 1* discover about Saturn? ........................................................................

**67.** What would Pam rather do in the morning? ...........................................................................

**68.** What is the minimum height requirement for the New York City police force? ........................

**69.** What is one way microchips are used in cars? ......................................................................

**70.** Which country accounts for 70% of the world's gold production? ...........................................

**71.** What will the Department of Sanitation have done before the circus arrives? ........................

**72.** Why won't Mark be able to pick Tina up from work? ..............................................................

**73.** About how many women will be running in the marathon? ......................................................

**74.** What did the couple want to have for dinner? ........................................................................

**75.** What did Joe Watkins say? ....................................................................................................

**76.** Where are the first negotiations going to be held? ................................................................

**77.** Melissa had refused to see Don again. What do you think she actually said? .......................

**78.** Why did Simon start calling Rachel "Cinderella?" ..................................................................

**79.** When you're in England, you call it a "biscuit." What do you call it in the United States? .......

**80.** Why did Mrs. Simmons want Yoshiko to write? ......................................................................